Swaps and Financial Engineering

A Self-Study Guide to Mastering and Applying Swaps and Financial Engineering

Coopers & Lybrand

PROBUS PUBLISHING COMPANY
Chicago, Illinois
Cambridge, England

First published by IFR Publishing, London, UK, 1992/1993

ISBN 1-55738-592-0

Printed in the United States of America

BB

2 3 4 5 6 7 8 9 0

Contents

Preface

Since its inception in the early 1980s the swaps market has experienced phonomenal growth and is now a market of over US$3 trillion in size. This exponential growth means that swaps are now used by most financial institutions and corporate treasuries. At present there are only 70 swaps houses recognised by the International Swaps Dealers Association (ISDA)—largely major players in the international capital markets. Yet, as demand for these products continues to increase, the market will surely experience further growth in both the size and in the number of players. Innovation in the marketplace may be dominated currently by a few sophisticated derivatives houses, but many more organizations are involved in the day-to-day activity.

A professional guide to understanding swaps is essential for the various participants—be they management, trainee traders, back office support, system designers, accountants, or corporate treasurers seeking to use swaps in asset management. The Workbook Series on Derivatives is an excellent and muchneeded contribution to helping those with an interest in swaps to understand the variety and complexity of today's market.

John S. Spences
Deputy Chief Executive
Barclays de Zoete Wedd
November 1992

Foreword

In October 1991 we published *The Financial Jungle—a guide to financial instruments* to help promote the understanding of financial instruments and to identify the risks and benefits to both designers and users. Our sponsorship of the Workbook Series on Derivatives continues this theme.

New, increasingly sophisticated and complex swaps products are being designed all the time. The pace of change has been so rapid that many supporting personnel as well as senior management have struggled to keep step with the risk, accounting, tax, and regulatory implications of these innovative products. Examples abound on what happens when organizations trade financial instruments without fully understanding how they are put together.

It is vital that the designers understand the accounting and tax implications of the financial instruments they are seeking to promote. Equally, it is important for the users of instruments to comprehend their economic rationale and effect to ensure all risks are identified before transactions are completed. We believe these workbooks are part of the answer. They are well structured and easy to follow guides on how swaps are designed and how they work. Divided into four volumes—*Interest Rate Swaps, Currency Swaps, Equity Swaps, and Swaps and Financial Engineering*—they are invaluable study aids.

Phil Rivett
Chairman, Securities and Commodities Group

Paul Reyniers
Chairman, Financial Risk Management Group

Coopers & Lybrand
November 1992

Introduction

'Financial engineering' emerged as one of the 'buzz' phrases of the 1980s. The phrase has been much used and abused. To the extent, this has been inevitable. Financial engineering as an identifiable discipline was not the result of invention but of evolution. Such imprecise origins made it difficult to define and the rapidity of its evolution compounded the problem. In this workbook, financial engineering is seen as being almost synonymous with swaps, which is the reason for making it the headline subject of the fourth workbook in the Workbook Series on Derivatives. Swaps are the essential tool of financial engineering (some may argue an equal case for options, which are undoubtedly very important, but only swaps are necessary and sufficient for financial engineering). It is no coincidence that the emergence of financial engineering was paralleled by the development of the swap market: the two processes were really one and the same. It was the development of swaps which powered financial engineering. Specifically, financial engineering progressed through the development of more complex swaps, in particular, asset and non-generic swaps. By placing asset and non-generic swaps in the context of financial engineering, it is hoped to provide some perspective on these types of swap and also some insight into the concrete nature of financial engineering.

Asset swaps represent a secondary stage in the development of the swap market. Swaps originated on the liability side of the capital markets as a means of 'new issue arbitrage'. In the early days of the swap market, only large transactions were economic and this meant swapping something on the scale of a Eurobond issue. Asset swaps were constrained by the relatively modest size of individual investments. However, as the swap market has matured, it has become more concentrated). It is also true that the techniques of swapping—in other words, of financial engineering—have become better understood and intermediaries more willing to customise assets for investors. Non-generic swaps are even more a reflection of the demand for customisation (of both assets and liabilities).

While asset and non-generic swaps overlap (many asset swaps are non-generic), the two types of swaps have been differentiated in this workbook because non-generic swaps involve an extra degree of engineering. In comparative terms, asset swaps can be seen as collections of individual instruments brought together for a specific purpose (to swap a specific asset), whereas non-generic swaps are combinations of individual instruments into structures which constitute discrete instruments in themselves, often designed for general use. The only disadvantage of this approach has been that the workbook has had to neglect looser types of liability swap structure (the liability equivalent to asset swaps). However, these are less important and form a less coherent area than either asset or non-generic swaps.

Richard Comotto
June 1993

How to use this workbook

The workbook is designed as a self-study programme. It has therefore been structured to guide the reader systematically through the subject and provides practical examples and case studies throughout to illustrate key points. The sources of market information used by experienced swaps practitioners are summarised and examples have been included from both screen-based information services and market publications.

Those intending to use this workbook should be familiar with basic interest rate concepts and arithmetic, including forward-forward interest rates. However, the workbook ignores unnecessary technical complications in the form of alternative interest rate conventions. Knowledge of these conventions is vital in swap transactions, but is not specific to swaps and can be gained from a wide number of other sources. As the asset swaps and non-generic swaps which are the subject of this workbook are complex structures, it is recommended that readers first make themselves familiar with generic swaps. These are covered in the workbooks *Interest Rate Swaps* and *Currency Swaps*.

A set of questions and answers is provided at the end of Part Two and Part Three to enable the reader to test and monitor progress. To further facilitate the planning of study time, an estimate for the time needed to complete each chapter and set of exercises is given. Instructions for marking the exercises are set at the back of the workbook. Both the timing and marking system are based on actual tests given to a representative sample of readers.

The workbook has been designed primarily for those with little or no experience of swaps, particularly where there is an urgent need to know. Experienced swap dealers and sales staff, however, may also find it valuable, not only in organising the training of their junior staff, but also when making swaps presentations to clients who require a degree of familiarisation with the subject.

Other workbooks in the series:

Interest Rate Swaps
Currency Swaps
Equity Swaps

For further information on the workbook series, please call Probus Publishing at 1-800-PROBUS-1 or 1-312-868-1100.

1 Financial engineering

What is financial engineering?

Definition	**Financial engineering is a multi-disciplinary approach to the management of risk and return which involves the use of derivative instruments to decompose standard financial transactions into their elements and then synthesise these elements into innovative cross-market structures customised to the particular requirements of counterparties.**

The term 'financial engineering' was coined in the mid 1980s, among London investment banks, to describe an emerging body of related risk management techniques which were being applied across traditional departmental boundaries. In many banks, expertise in these techniques has been brought together in specialist financial engineering groups. Indeed, financial engineering is now often described as a 'discipline'.

Financial engineering is the product of several parallel developments:

■ **Financial innovation** and the emergence during the 1980s of derivative instruments, which provide the basic tools for financial engineering, in particular, swaps and other over-the-counter (OTC) derivatives.

■ The emergence of both derivative instruments and financial engineering has only been possible because of the development of new **information technology**, in particular, the PC and spreadsheet software. These innovations have provided a fast and flexible means of managing the large volumes of information which are necessary to construct complex transactions. Other innovations, mainly in the field of tele-communications, have reduced the cost of generating and delivering the information which is the raw material of the process. Lower costs have in turn increased the availability of information, which has extended the range of opportunities for financial engineering to exploit.

- An important force behind the emergence of financial engineering has been the trend towards **liberalisation** of financial markets which began at the end of the 1970s. The removal of official barriers has permitted the cross-market activity that characterises financial engineering. The competition it has unleashed has encouraged the process. However, care needs to be taken in attributing cause and effect in this area. Financial engineering has played a part in encouraging liberalisation by undermining the effectiveness of regulation. On the other hand, liberalisation has a negative effect on financial engineering, since administrative distortions like regulation create the anomalies which provide many of the arbitrage opportunities for financial engineering.

- The increasing **volatility** of prices during the 1970s and 1980s increased both the need to hedge risk and the opportunities for taking risk. Financial engineering is the product of the growing sophistication of risk management techniques.

- Financial engineering reflects the more rigorous application of the **scientific method** to finance, in particular, analysis into elements and empirical testing (in the form of financial modelling and sensitivity analyses). This methodological change has itself been reflected in the greater use of quantitative techniques and the development of a corpus of financial theory (the classic example being the options pricing theory of Black and Scholes). It has also been seen in a trend towards the recruitment of staff with scientific rather than financial training, in particular, physicists and mechanical engineers. The popular name for a financial engineer — 'rocket scientist' — may therefore sometimes be literally true.

What does financial engineering do?

The nature of financial engineering can be seen more clearly by examining the key parts of its definition:

Multi-disciplinary approach

Financial engineering straddles several traditional financial markets. It is also frequently used to exploit anomalies in the tax, accounting and regulatory frameworks within which markets operate. Financial engineering is therefore conducted by 'teams', which bring together traders, financial analysts, syndication staff, corporate finance officers, lawyers, tax specialists, accountants, mathematicians, statisticians, compliance officers, programmers and other specialists.

Derivative instruments

Financial engineering usually involves the application of derivative instruments, in particular, swaps and options. Swaps are the single most important tool of financial engineering. It is the exchange of cash flows which takes place through a swap which is the means by which financial transactions (eg, debt) are decomposed into their constituent elements (eg, interest rate, currency and prepayment risks) and also the means by which these elements are reassembled, in different permutations, for synthesis into new types of transaction. The swap mechanism is available, not just in the obvious form of interest rate and currency swaps, but also as forward rate agreements (FRAs), futures and foreign exchange instruments. Thus, FRAs involve a net exchange of fixed interest (at the Contract Reference Rate) against floating interest (at the Settlement Rate). Short-term interest rate futures are equivalent to FRAs, but are standardised and exchange-traded (with interest rates being implied rather than quoted directly). Foreign exchange instruments are types of currency swap.

Decomposing into elements

The process of decomposition is commonly referred to as **unbundling** and the constituent parts are often called **building blocks**. The ability to decompose standard financial transactions into common elements is the basis not only of financial engineering, but also of **portfolio management**, in which diverse transactions are managed in aggregate by breaking them down into simple common elements which can be more easily hedged.

Elements

Various attempts have been made to define and classify the elements themselves. Table 1 sets out one of the first efforts, produced by a central bank study group at the Bank for International Settlements (BIS) in the seminal *Recent Innovations in International Banking* (April 1986). One of the most extensive attempts is by J D Finnerty in 'Financial Engineering in Corporate Finance', *Financial Management* (Winter 1988). However, it is rather easier to break financial instruments down into simpler instruments, rather than their pure elements. In practice, all financial instruments can be seen as being composed of:

■ forward contracts

■ option contracts

■ a combination of the two.

Synthesis

A classification of instruments in terms of the forwards and options which underlie them is reproduced in Box 1 from Das, *Swap Financing*, which is published by IFR.

Having unbundled a standard financial transaction into its elements, financial engineers then recombine the elements in new permutations as new types of transaction. This is the process of synthesis, also known as **repackaging**. The results are often labelled as **synthetic** or **hybrid** instruments.

Table 1: A classification of innovations

Innovation	Price-risk transferring	Credit-risk transferring	Liquidity-enhancing	Credit-enhancing	Equity-generating
A On-balance sheet					
Adjustable-rate mortgages	X				
Floating-rate loans	X				
Back-to-back loans	X				
Asset sales without recourse		X			
Loan swaps		X			
Securitised assets		X	X		
Transferable loan contracts		X	X		
Sweep accounts and other cash management techniques			X		
Negotiable money market instruments			X		
Money market mutual funds			X		
Zero coupon bonds				X	
'Junk' bonds				X	
Equity participation financing				X	
Mandatory convertible debentures					X
B Off-balance sheet					
Futures	X				
Options and loan caps	X				
Swaps	X			X	
Forward rate agreements	X				
Letters of credit		X			
Note issuance facilities	X	X	X		
Credit-enhancing guarantees on securities		X	X		

Box 1: The elements of financial engineering

A forward contract obligates the purchaser to buy a given asset on a specified date at a known price (known, usually, as the forward price). This forward price is specified at the time the contract is entered into. If at maturity the actual price is higher than the forward price, the contract owner will make a profit; if the price is lower, the owner suffers a loss.

A forward contract entailing the sale of a given asset on a specified date in the future at a known forward price is also feasible, representing the offsetting side of a forward purchase. In this case, the payoffs for the forward seller are clearly reversed.

In the case of forward contracts in capital markets, the underlying asset will usually be either a security or a specified amount of foreign currency. Where the asset is a security, its price will reflect interest rates. Consequently, a forward contract on such an asset would essentially operate functionally as a forward contract on interest rates. Similarly, where the underlying commodity is a specified amount of the foreign currency, the forward contract essentially represents a forward currency contract.

From a functional perspective, a futures contract is identical to a forward contract in that a futures contract also obligates its owner to purchase or sell a specified asset at a specified forward price on the contract maturity date.

The major difference between futures and forward contracts relates to the institutional structure of the two markets. In the case of futures contracts, the underlying asset to be traded is usually homogenised through a process of standardisation and specification of nominated exercise dates (usually four per year). This is usually designed to enable the futures market to become relatively liquid. An additional difference of significance is the use of a futures exchange or clearing house which acts as a counterparty to each transaction. This is designed not only to facilitate liquidity but to reduce the likelihood of credit or default risk through a process of performance bonds, involving the posting of deposits and margins. Technically, a futures contract is a forward contract which is settled daily with a new forward contract being written simultaneously.

The relationship between interest rate swap contracts and forward contracts derives from the fact that, in effect, the swap contract is a series of forward contracts combined. An interest rate swap entails the exchange of specified cash flows determined by reference to two different interest rates. An interest rate swap can be represented by a series of cash inflows in return for a series of cash outflows. This contractual arrangement can be decomposed into a portfolio of simpler single payment contracts, which can in turn be decomposed into a series of forward contracts. Utilising this approach, it is possible to restate an interest rate swap as a series of implicit forward contracts on interest rates.

As noted above, an FRA contract is essentially a market in forward interest rates, in effect forward contracts on interest rates. Consequently, FRAs are logically linked to interest rate swaps in a manner identical to the linkage between forward contracts and interest rate swaps.

A forward contract, as specified above, entails an obligation to buy or sell the stated asset. In contrast, an option contract gives the purchaser the right, but not the obligation, to purchase or sell an asset. A call option gives the owner the right to purchase an asset while a put option gives the purchaser the right to sell the asset. In both cases, the purchase price or selling price is specified at the time the option contract is originated. This price is usually referred to as the exercise price. The financial price of the asset, as in the case of forward contracts, can be an interest rate or a currency exchange rate.

The purchaser of a call option contract has the right to purchase the asset at the exercise price. Consequently if the price of the asset rises above the exercise price, then the value of the option also goes up. However, because the option contract does not obligate the purchaser to purchase the asset if the price falls, the value of the option does not fall by the same amount as the price declines. A similar but reverse logic applies in the case of put options.

The pay-off profile of the party who has sold (written or granted) the call or put option is different. In contrast to the purchaser of the option, the seller of the option has the obligation to perform. For example, if the holder of the option elects to exercise her or his option to purchase the asset, the seller of the option is obligated to sell the asset.

The relationship between option contracts and swap transactions operates at a number of levels:

■   the relationship between option contracts and forward contracts;

■   the relationship between option contracts and interest rate swaps.

It can be demonstrated that there are at least two inter-related linkages between options and forward contracts:

■ A call option can be replicated by continuously adjusting or managing dynamically a portfolio of securities or forward contracts on the underlying asset (for example, securities or foreign exchange) and riskless securities or cash. As the price of the asset rises, the call option equivalent portfolio would contain an increasing proportion of the assets or forward contracts. As the financial price of the asset decreases, the call option equivalent portfolio would reduce its holding of the assets of forward contracts.

■ Option contracts can be used to replicate forward contracts through a relationship known as put call parity. In terms of this relationship, the simultaneous purchase of a call option and the sale of a put option is equivalent to a forward purchase while the sale of a call option simultaneously combined with the purchase of a put option is equivalent to a forward sale.

These two levels of linkage between options and forward contracts imply a natural structural and economic relationship between the two instruments. In turn, option contracts impose a similar influence on interest rate swaps indirectly through their relationship with forward or futures contracts.

More directly, as noted above, options may have a direct relationship to interest rate swaps insofar as an interest rate swap can be characterised as a portfolio of purchased and sold options. This, of course, reflects the fact that an interest rate swap can be characterised as a series of forward contracts while forward contracts can be replicated through option contracts.

Swap instruments, such as caps, floors and collars are, in effect, a series of option contracts. This means that they are directly equivalent to underlying option contracts and consequently would enjoy a similar relationship to both forward and futures contracts or their customised equivalent FRAs as well as to interest rate swaps.

The discussion to date has confined itself to instruments in a single currency. However, the analysis is capable of extension to a multi-currency situation. A currency swap between two currencies is equivalent to a portfolio of currency forwards and futures or, alternatively, a portfolio of purchased and sold currency options. The currency forwards and currency options themselves are, first, linked to each other through option put call parity and replicating portfolio relationships, and, second, to the interest rate swap, forward and/or futures and option markets in their respective currencies.

This complex inter-relationship between swap, forward and option markets is illustrated in the figure below both in a single and multiple currency setting.

As illustrated, the capacity for swap transactions to be essentially dismembered into the basic constituent forward and option contracts is clearly evident. The ability to decompose swaps is not only elegant but highly useful for a number of reasons:

■ the structural relationships allow the specific elements of individual transactions to be separated and recombined to create new instruments. This is particularly important in more complex liability and asset swap structures;

■ the inter-relationships form the basis of pricing swap transactions. The established technology of pricing forward and option contracts provides the basis for the pricing and economic analysis of swaps;

■ the decomposition process also facilitates the trading and hedging of swap transactions where financial institutions make markets in these instruments.

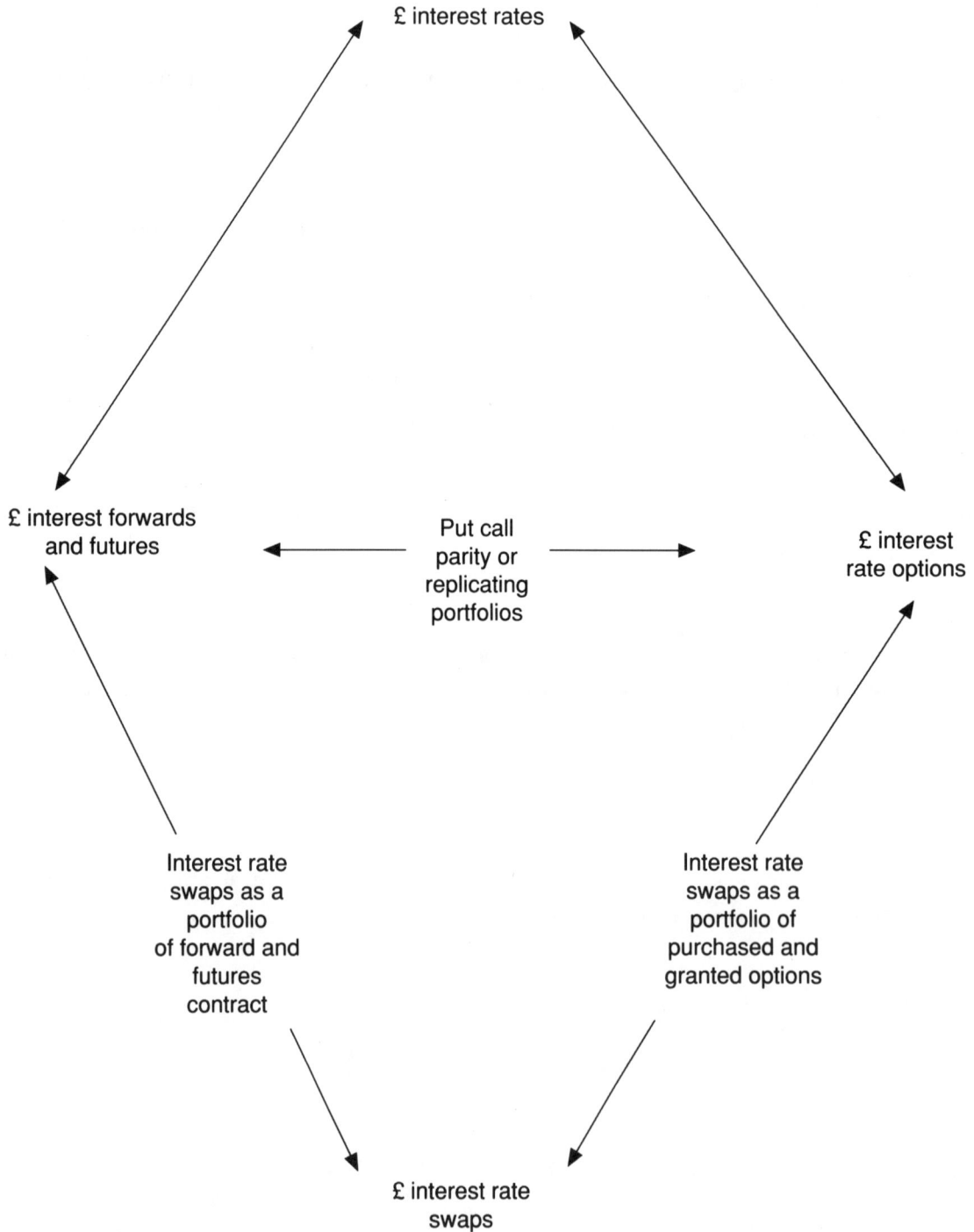

Swap, forward and option market inter-relationships

£ interest rates

£ interest forwards
and futures

Put call
parity or
replicating
portfolios

£ interest
rate options

Interest rate
swaps as a
portfolio
of forward and
futures
contract

Interest rate
swaps as a
portfolio of
purchased and
granted options

£ interest rate
swaps

£ interest rates

£ interest rate
forwards and
futures

£ interest
rate options

£ interest
rate swaps

£: US$
currency
forwards and
futures

£: US$ currency swaps
as a portfolio
of £: US$ currency
forwards and futures

£: US$
spot exchange
rate

Put call
parity or replicating
portfolios

A$: US$
currency
swaps

£: US$ currency swaps
as a portfolio
of purchased and
granted £: US$ options

£: US$
currency options

US$ interest
rate swaps

US$ interest rate
forwards and futures

US$ interest
rate options

US$ interest rates

Source: *Swap Financing*, Satyajit Das, pages 20–24

Innovation

The process of innovation takes place when a new and broader perspective is taken on old problems. Financial engineering seeks such a perspective in order to identify common elements in traditionally different markets. A large part of the process therefore involves the search for new relationships or at least behavioural correlations. The consequent number-crunching has acquired the name 'quant' for researchers in financial engineering teams.

Cross-market structures

As noted already, financial engineering takes place across the boundaries which separate traditional markets. Indeed, the fundamental purpose of financial engineering is to provide a broader perspective which helps identify opportunities for the transfer of risk and arbitrage between different markets. An important consequence of the cross-market activities of financial engineering is to accelerate the integration of markets, which should become more efficient in terms of their ability to match the supply and demand for money, and their transactions costs.

Structures

The transactions which are synthesised by financial engineers can be quite complex. This may reflect the unusual nature of the opportunity being exploited or the extent of customisation to the particular requirements of counterparties. However, given that all financial instruments can be broken down into forward contracts or options or both, even basic instruments like swaps can be regarded as products of financial engineering in themselves. Financial engineering can therefore be viewed at different levels:

- the engineering of sometimes quite complex instruments into even more complex structures, usually for a special purpose. Asset swaps fall into this category and are examined in *Part Two*.

- the engineering of generally quite simple instruments into complex structures which constitute discrete instruments in themselves, usually for general use. These are called non-generic swaps and are described in *Part Three*.

2 Asset swaps

What is an asset swap?

Definition	An asset swap is an interest rate or currency swap which is attached to an asset.

The distinguishing feature of an asset swap is the fact that it is linked to an *asset*. This means that, whereas liability swaps are used by borrowers, asset swaps are used by *investors*. It also means that cash flows come *into* an asset swap, whereas they go out of a liability swap. However, the structure of the swap mechanism in an asset swap is no different to that in a liability swap. The structures are compared in Diagram 1.

Diagram 1: Comparing the structure of asset and liability swaps

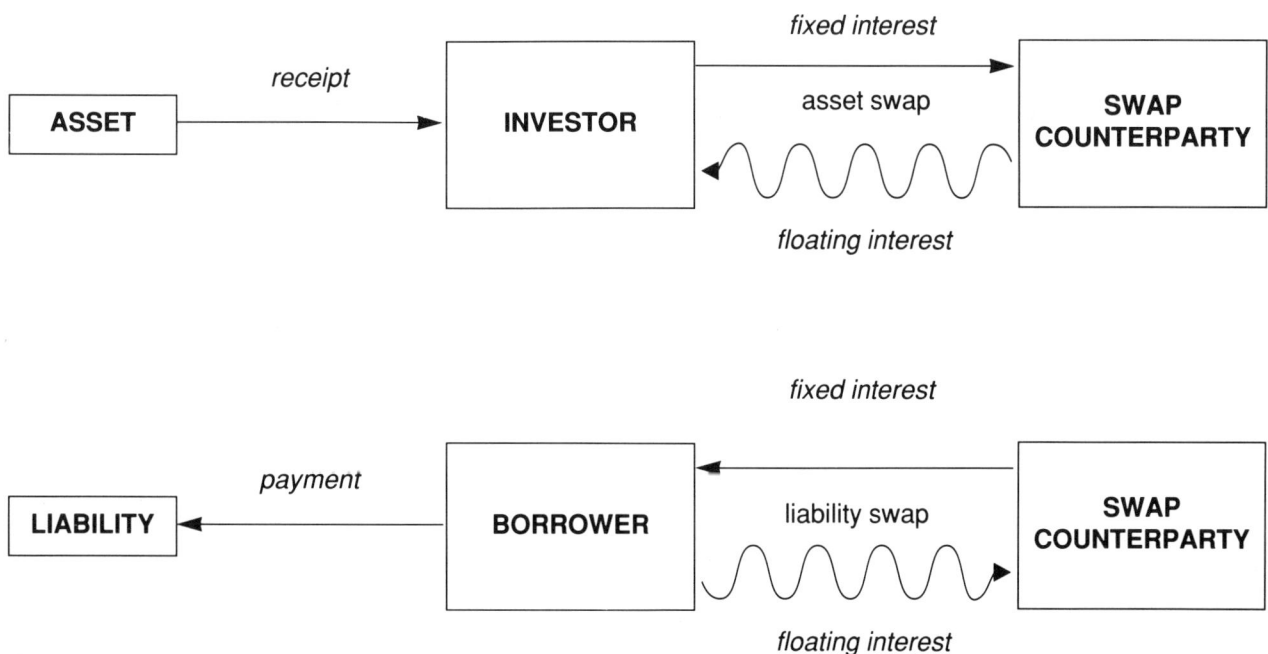

Like liability swaps, asset swaps can be interest rate or currency swaps. Asset swaps also frequently have *non-generic* structures, in order to re-order cash flows to match investors' requirements (see also *Part Three*). The process of combining swaps and assets is part of the general activity of *financial engineering* which was discussed in *Part One*.

Asset swaps appeared later than liability swaps. This sequence of development reflected the economics of the early swap market. Initially, only large swaps were economic. In practice, this meant new issue arbitrage by borrowers swapping against complete Eurobond issues. Investors, on the other hand, tend to transact in more modest amounts than borrowers, buying and selling only parts of issues. However, over time, improved technology has led to the development of sophisticated techniques such as warehousing and portfolio management, which have allowed intermediaries to act as market-makers in swaps. Together with increased competition as the swap market has matured and as swaps have become less proprietary, this has reduced the unit cost of swapping and the minimum deal size down to amounts suitable for swapping assets.

What do asset swaps do?

Asset swaps and investors

Given the similarity in structure of asset and liability swaps, investors can use swaps for the same reasons as borrowers:

■   **Risk management:**

—   *Take* risk, by converting cash flows from one interest rate basis or currency to a new one.

—   *Hedge* against risk, by converting cash flows from one interest basis or currency to an opposite one.

—   *Hedge* against risk, by portfolio *diversification*. Swaps can be used to create assets for investors not otherwise available in the markets, from assets which are readily available. Swaps can be used to diversify, not just interest and exchange rate risks, but also *credit risk*. This is because the scope for portfolio diversification in some asset markets is limited by the narrow range of creditworthy names issuing in that market: asset swaps can introduce new names who only issue in other markets by swapping assets from those other markets. Asset swaps also provide a means of hedging credit risk by *asset-backing:* the asset being swapped is used as a pledge to collateralise the asset swap (this involves a special type of asset swap structure — a so-called 'repackaged security' — which is described in a later section).

—   *Hedge* against *liquidity risk*, by re-ordering cash flows from an asset to better match investor requirements. Such **cash flow adjustment** is performed by swaps with off-market prices, which allow cash flows to be redistributed over time, typically, between upfront cash payments and regular interest payments.

■   **Return management:** to *arbitrage* between the same interest rates in different markets in order to make a profit from any price anomalies which can be used to enhance the overall rate of return on an investment.

Asset swaps and intermediaries

Asset swaps also have numerous advantages for intermediaries:

- Illiquid or underperforming assets can be shifted from trading books.

- The price of poorly-performing issues can be supported.

- By absorbing a certain asset or class of assets, room for new issues can be created.

- Additional fee income can be earned. Moreover, as assets are provided to investors by swapping existing assets, this income does not require an intermediary to take new balance sheet risk (eg, underwriting new issues).

- Some intermediaries have been accused of using asset swaps (in the form of issues of 'repackaged securities' — see the section 'Types of Asset Swaps') to boost their standing in league tables of new bond issues.

- As illustrated in Diagram 2, asset swap arbitrages can provide the opposite side to liability swap arbitrages, assisting the management of swap portfolios by market-makers, thereby indirectly supporting market liquidity.

Diagram 2: The match between asset and liability swap arbitrages

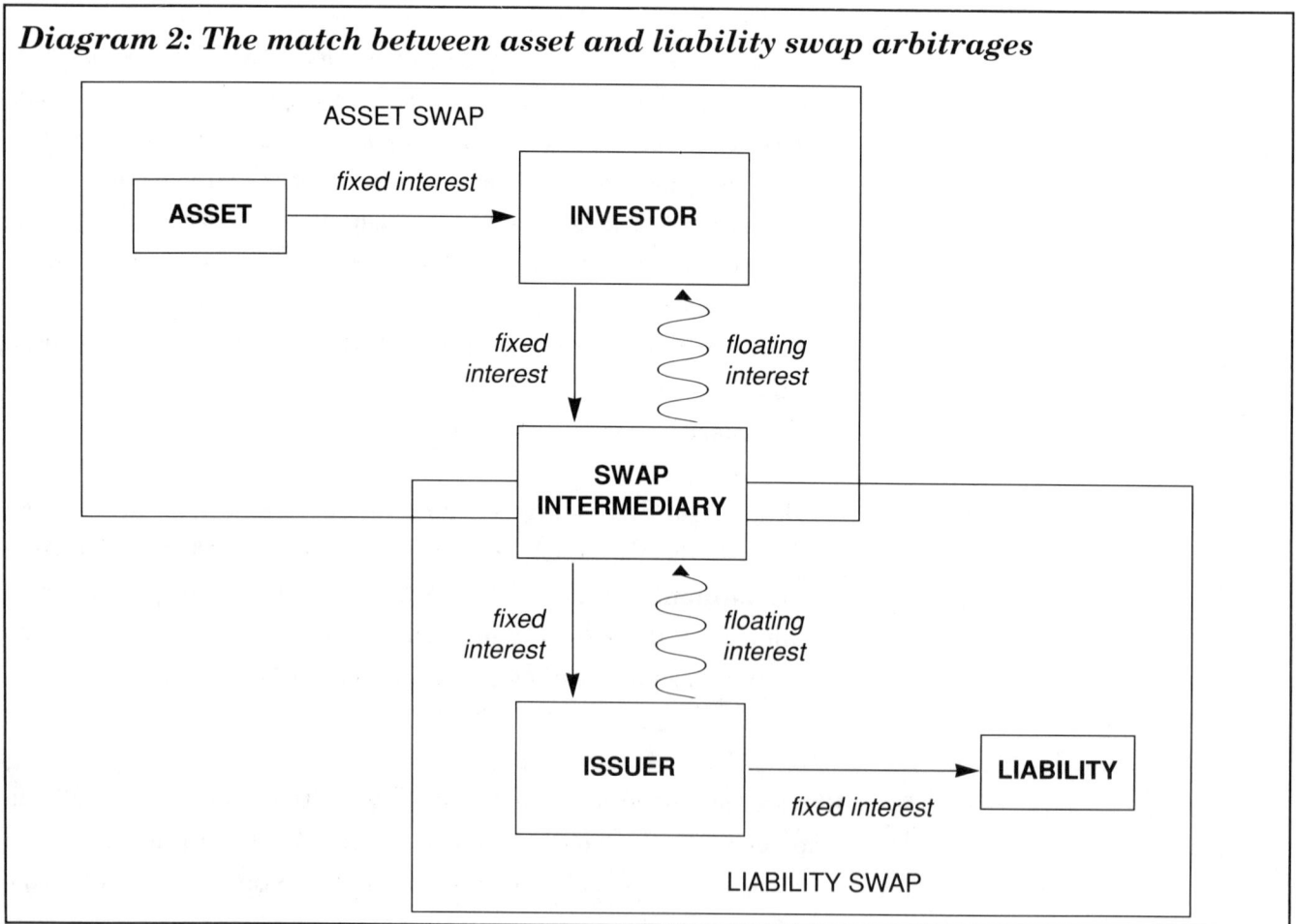

Using asset swaps

Risk management with asset swaps: taking and hedging interest and exchange rate risk

Asset swaps are used to manage interest rate or currency risk, like liability swaps, in order to anticipate changes in interest or exchange rates. However, whereas borrower-driven liability swaps are used to take the risk that rates will fall or hedge against the risk that rates will rise, investor-driven asset swaps are used to take the risk that rates will rise or hedge against the risk that rates will fall. These basic uses of asset swaps are described in the earlier Workbooks in the IFR Swap Series — *Interest Rate Swaps* and *Currency Swaps*.

Risk management with asset swaps: diversification of credit risk

As noted already, asset swaps can be used to increase the range of assets available to investors and thereby facilitate the diversification of their portfolios. Swaps can be used to facilitate the diversification of credit risk by expanding the range of creditworthy names issuing in particular markets by swapping assets from other markets. For example, FRNs can be created from fixed interest bonds issued by corporate borrowers, adding diversity to the traditional issuer base, which is dominated by banks. An example using currency asset swaps is the classic swapping of World Bank debt from Swiss francs and Deutsche marks into dollars. This prime issuer traditionally preferred to tap low-yielding currencies and avoided high-yielding currencies. In 1982, the first major publicised currency swap provided dollar investors with World Bank risk (this swap is described in detail in the earlier Workbook — *Currency Swaps*).

The use of asset swaps to hedge credit risk by *asset-backing* is described in the later section 'Types of Asset Swaps', which explains the 'repackaging' structure used to collateralise asset swaps.

Risk management with asset swaps: cash flow adjustment

Swaps are frequently used to re-order the cash flows on assets to better match investors' requirements. Investors may require highly customised cash flows, but there are also a number of standard cash flow adjustments which are widely used.

*Adjusting for accrued
interest and premiums
and discounts.*

For tax and accounting reasons, investors tend to have a preference for assets on which interest income is paid at current market rates and not as capital, in other words, securities *without:*

■ **accrued interest:** so-called 'clean' securities;

■ **premium** or **discount** between face value and purchase price, and therefore with a coupon rate equal to the current market yield: securities priced at par.

In practice, however, it is usually difficult to find such assets when required:

■ Assets without accrued interest would have to be purchased at issue or on a coupon payment date.

■ Assets are only usually priced at par at issue and sometimes not even then.

These problems mean that the cash flows on underlying assets usually have to be adjusted in order to produce asset swaps which can appeal to investors. Thus:

■ Any payment of accrued interest by the investor when it purchases the underlying asset has to be immediately compensated by the intermediary through an upfront cash payment to the investor. The intermediary will recoup this payment of accrued interest, and the cost of funding it until a coupon is actually paid, by subtracting a margin from the floating interest which it pays to the investor through the swap. The margin is calculated by amortising the accrued interest over the remaining life of the asset.

■ Any premium or discount on the price of underlying asset when it is purchased by the investor needs to be eliminated by the intermediary:

— A *premium* is eliminated by the intermediary making an equivalent cash payment (usually upfront, but sometimes back-ended) to the investor as compensation: in net terms, the investor ends up paying for the asset at par. However, the intermediary recoups the payment to the investor by reducing the interest paid to the investor. As the coupon paid by the asset cannot be reduced, the necessary reduction in the interest paid to the investor is achieved by adjusting the cash flows through the swap. This is usually done by subtracting a margin from the floating interest which the intermediary pays to the investor through the swap.

— A *discount* is eliminated by the investor making an equivalent cash payment (usually upfront, but sometimes back-ended) to the intermediary as compensation: in net terms, the investor ends up paying for ·the asset at par. However, the payment to the intermediary is repaid by increasing the interest paid to the investor. As the coupon paid by the asset cannot be increased, the necessary increase in the interest paid to the investor is achieved by adjusting the cash flows through the swap. This is usually done by adding a margin to the floating interest which the intermediary pays to the investor through the swap.

The margins required to offset the cash payments made to eliminate premiums or discounts are calculated by amortising the amount of a premium or discount over the remaining life of the asset.

Adjusting for mismatches between coupons and the swap rate

Investors not only prefer assets without accrued interest and priced at par, but also asset swaps in which the coupon paid on the asset is equal to the fixed interest paid through the swap. If the coupon rate and swap rate differ, an investor is exposed to **reinvestment risk**: uncertainty about the total return on the swapped asset, because the future interest rates at which a net interest gain can be invested or a net interest loss funded are unknown in advance. Reinvestment risk in asset swaps is solved by setting the swap rate at the same level as the coupon rate on the asset, which will mean the swap rate is off-market (such swaps are called *premium* or *discount swaps* and are described in *Part Three*). However, the counterparty which is disadvantaged by this off-market swap rate — the payer, if the off-market rate is above current swap rates; the receiver, if it is below — must be compensated by either:

■ a cash payment (usually upfront, but sometimes back-ended) from the other counterparty;

■ an adjustment in the form of a margin to the floating interest through the swap.

The cash payment required to offset an off-market swap rate is the net present value (NPV) of the series of differences between a stream of interest payments calculated at the coupon rate and a stream calculated at the current swap rate. The alternative of a margin against the floating interest paid through the swap is calculated by amortising the NPV over the remaining life of the asset.

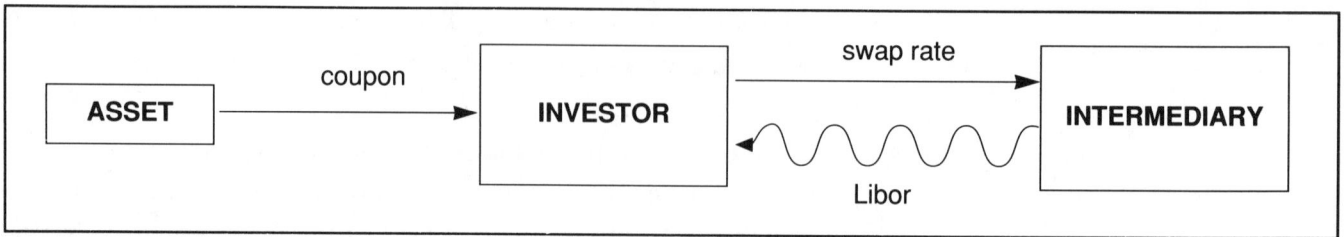

Table 2: Summary of standard cash flow adjustments

Cash flow problems	Current market yield compared to coupon on asset	Swap rate compared to coupon on asset	Cash flow adjustments
Accrued interest			Cash payment *to* investor *and* margin *below* Libor
Asset priced at premium or discount	HIGHER (Asset at discount)		Cash payment **from** investor *and* margin **over** Libor
	LOWER (Asset at premium)		Cash payment **to** investor *and* margin **below** Libor
Mismatch between coupon and swap rate creating reinvestment risk		LOWER	**Increase** swap rate (premium swap) *and* margin **over** Libor *or* cash payment **to** investor
		HIGHER	**Decrease** swap rate (discount swap) *and* margin **below** Libor *or* cash payment **from** investor

The cash flow adjustments which are required to deal with the problems of assets priced at premiums or discounts, and mismatches between the coupon on assets and the swap rate, are summarised in Table 1.

An example

Consider the following asset and swap:

remaining life	= 5 years 275 days
face value	= £100m
dirty price	= 96.16 (rounded)
accrued interest	= £3.082m
clean price	= 93.07 (rounded)
coupon	= 12.50% per annum
current market yield	= 14.30% per annum
coupon payment	= annual
annual basis	= 365 days
next coupon	= 275 days
swap rate (5 years 275 days)	= 14.30% per annum

A simple asset swap structure using this asset and swap is illustrated in Diagram 3.

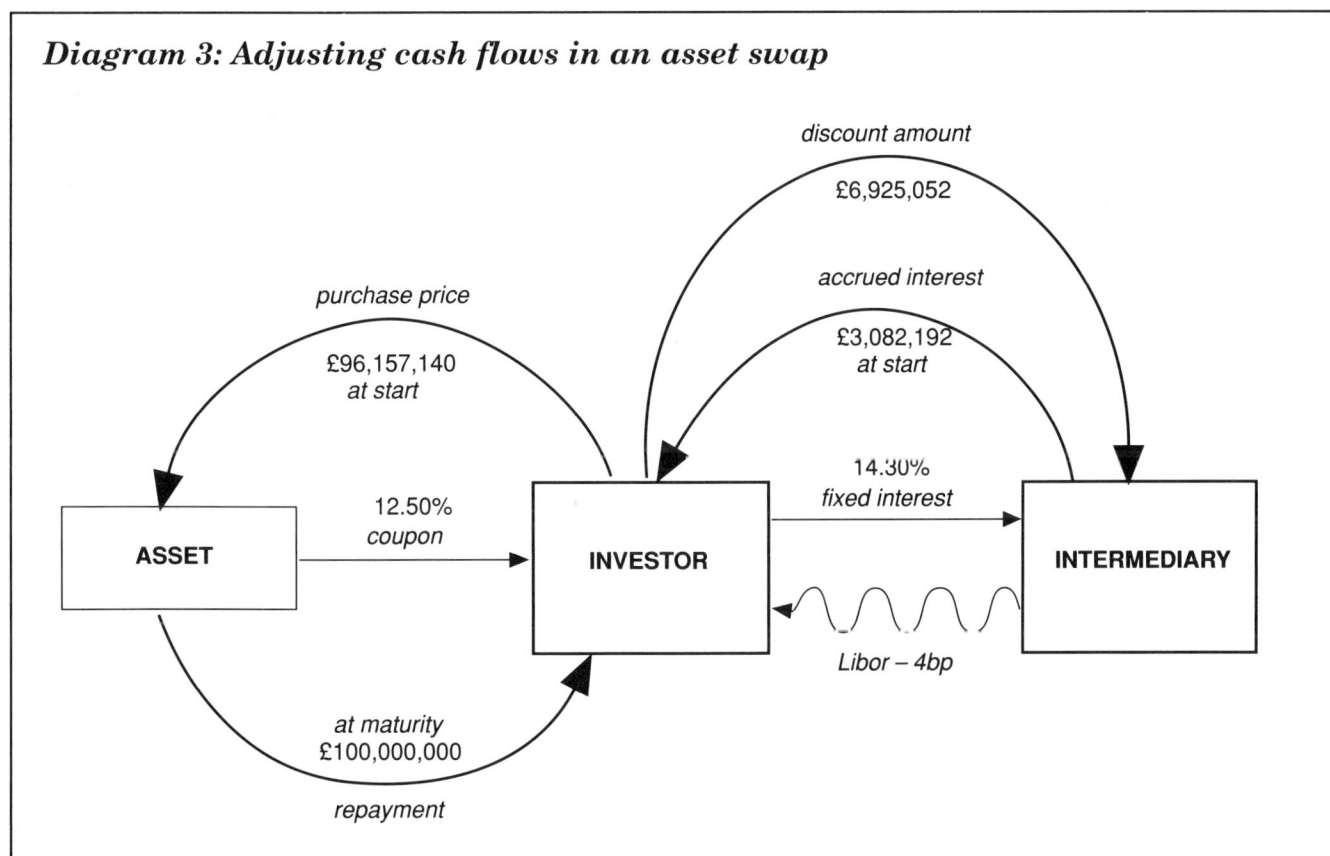

Diagram 3: Adjusting cash flows in an asset swap

The asset swap is created in the following steps:

■ The investor buys an amount of the asset with a face value of £100,000,000 for a dirty price of £96,157,140, which includes accrued interest of:

£100,000,000 x 12.5/100 x 90/365 = £3,082,192

■ The investor puts on a coupon swap with a notional principal amount of £100,000,000.

■ The swap intermediary compensates the investor for the accrued interest which it has paid in the dirty price of the asset (£3,082,192), with an equivalent upfront cash payment. However, the intermediary recoups this payment of accrued interest, and the cost of funding it for the 275 days until the next coupon payment, by subtracting a margin from the floating interest paid to the investor through the swap. The margin can be determined using a bond calculator. This example uses the standard bond calculator notation:

n	= number of years to maturity
PV	= price
PMT	= coupon
FV	= face value
i	= yield to maturity

Assuming a cost of funding equal to the current swap rate of 14.30% per annum, the margin is calculated by amortising the amount of the accrued interest over the remaining life of the asset (5 years and 275 days):

n	= 5.753 years (5 years 275 days)
PV	= −3.082192
FV	= 0
i	= 14.30%

which gives a negative margin of:

PMT	= 0.82%

■ The discount on the asset which the investor has bought is offset by the investor making an equivalent upfront cash payment to the intermediary. The intermediary repays this payment, and the cost of funding it, by adding a margin to the floating interest paid to the investor through the swap. Assuming a cost of funding equal to the current swap rate of 14.30% per annum, the margin is calculated by amortising the amount of the discount over the remaining life of the asset (5 years and 275 days):

n	= 5.753 years (5 years 275 days)
PV	= –6.925052
FV	= 0
i	= 14.30%

which gives a positive margin of:

PMT	= 1.84%

■ Finally, in order to eliminate the reinvestment risk caused by the mismatch between the coupon rate (12.50%) received by the investor on the asset and the swap rate (14.30%) paid through the swap, the swap is priced at an off-market swap rate equal to the coupon. As this is lower than the current swap rate, the intermediary will lose interest income and will recoup its shortfall by subtracting a margin from the floating interest paid to the investor through the swap. The margin is calculated by amortising the NPV of the series of differences between an interest stream calculated at the coupon rate and an interest stream calculated at the swap rate over the remaining life of the asset (5 years and 275 days). The calculation of this NPV is set out in Table 3.

Table 3: Calculating the NPV of the coupon-swap rate mismatch

| Period after purchase of asset (years) | Fixed interest payments through swap at: | | Differentials (A) – (B) | Present value of differentials |
	Current swap rate of 14.30% pa (A)	Off-market swap rate of 12.50% pa (B)		
0.753	10,773,973	12,500,000	−1,726,027	−1,560,681
1.753	14,300,000	12,500,000	+1,800,000	+1,423,944
2.753	14,300,000	12,500,000	+1,800,000	+1,245,795
3.753	14,300,000	12,500,000	+1,800,000	+1,089,934
4.753	14,300,000	12,500,000	+1,800,000	+953,573
5.753	14,300,000	12,500,000	+1,800,000	+834,272
	NPV of differentials in interest streams			+3,986,837

It is important to note here that the interest payment made through the swap on the first coupon date during the asset swap is for a full interest period. This is in order to match the full coupon received by the investor on the asset on the same date.

Assuming a cost of funding equal to the current swap rate of 14.30% per annum, amortising the NPV of £3,986,837:

n   = 5.753 years (5 years 275 days)
PV   = −3.986837
FV   = 0
i   = 14.30%

gives a negative margin of:

PMT = 1.06%

Assuming a floating interest rate index of Libor, the margin against the Libor paid to the investor through the swap is:

cost of accrued interest	−0.82%
cost of discount	+1.84%
cost of off-market swap rate	−1.06%
margins +/- Libor	−0.04%

Return management with asset swaps: arbitrage

The basic use of asset swaps in arbitrage involves swapping either from fixed to floating interest or vice versa.

Fixed to floating asset swaps

In Diagram 4, an asset is being swapped from a fixed to a floating interest basis. The arbitrage is between the higher fixed interest received on the asset and the lower fixed interest paid out through the swap. The resulting arbitrage profits are used to enhance the net floating interest return received by the investor.

Diagram 4: Arbitraging with an asset swap — from fixed to floating interest

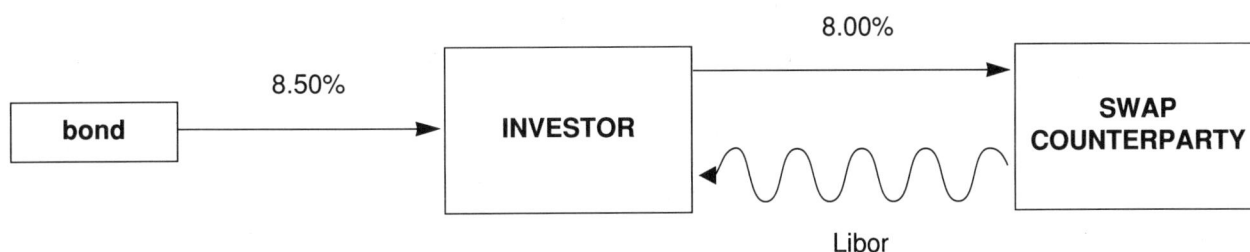

Receipts	fixed interest on asset	8.50%pa	
	floating interest through swap	Libor	arbitrage
Payments	fixed interest through swap	8.00%pa	
Net receipts	floating interest	Libor + 50bp	

All interest rates are quoted on the same basis

Swapping from fixed to floating interest is by far the most common direction in which assets are swapped. This bias is illustrated in Diagram 5 (although for 'repackaged' asset swap structures only — see the section 'Types of Asset Swap'). The greater arbitrage opportunities available by swapping from fixed to floating interest reflects both the supply of assets to be swapped and the demand for assets once swapped:

■ The **supply** of assets suitable for swapping is, in practice, greatest in the fixed interest market. This is demonstrated by the range of examples of assets suitable for arbitrage given later in this section (see the paragraph on arbitrage opportunities). It is also evident in the fact, noted directly below, that floating interest assets have tended to be scarce.

■ The **demand** for swapped assets has come mainly from commercial banks:

— these institutions need to match their floating interest liabilities with floating interest assets, but have suffered a shortage of conventional floating interest loan assets as the trend towards borrowing directly from investors through issues of securities, rather than borrowing via intermediaries, eroded their historic customer base and credit demand was curtailed by the lending crises of the 1980s;

— specific demand came from commercial banks based in Japan and elsewhere which were seeking to expand their international activities during the 1980s, but lacked traditional international banking business: this was reflected in the fact that most asset swaps have been into floating interest US dollars from non-dollar Eurobonds;

— demand for asset swaps into floating interest was boosted when the supply of real FRNs was interrupted in 1986 as issuers exercised call options in order to refinance from alternative sources, particularly from the rapidly developing Eurocommercial paper market;

— the international capital adequacy requirements imposed under the Basle Agreement, together with the recession and related loan losses, have forced commercial banks to shift the focus of their strategies from asset growth to return-on-assets: this has attracted banks to the arbitrage profits from asset swaps and fee income from the financial engineering of structured transactions;

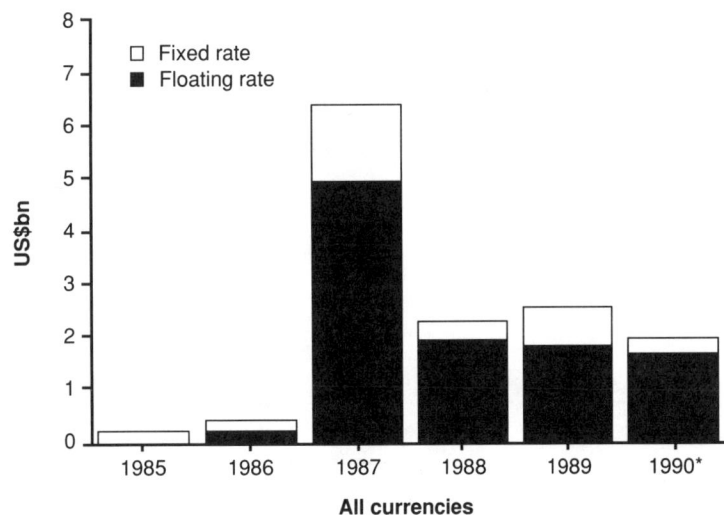

Diagram 5: Repackaged issues by type

* First three quarters

Source: Euromoney Bondware

Floating to fixed asset swaps

In Diagram 6, an asset is being swapped from a floating to a fixed interest basis. The arbitrage in this instance is between the higher floating interest received on the asset and the lower floating interest paid out through the swap. Floating interest assets usually return a yield above Libor, whereas the floating interest rate in swaps is normally flat Libor. The resulting arbitrage profits are used to enhance the net fixed interest return received by the investor.

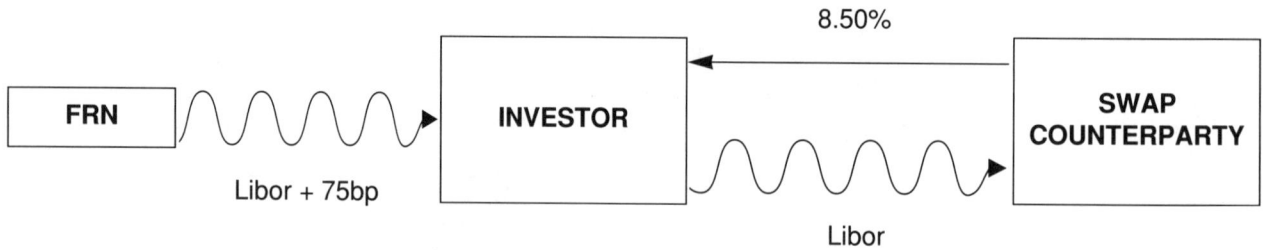

Diagram 6: Arbitraging with an asset swap — from floating to fixed interest

Receipts	fixed interest through swap	8.50%pa	
	floating interest on asset	Libor + 75bp	arbitrage
Payments	floating interest through swap	Libor	
Net receipts	fixed interest	9.25%pa	

All interest rates are quoted on the same basis

Asset swaps from floating interest have involved floating-rate notes (FRN), certificates of deposits (CD) and commercial paper (CP). The types of assets used are illustrated in Diagram 7 (although for 'repackaged' asset swap structures only). It can be seen that asset swaps of perpetual FRNs were particularly significant for a period after the crisis in this market in 1986.

Diagram 7: Repackaged issues by floating-rate source bond

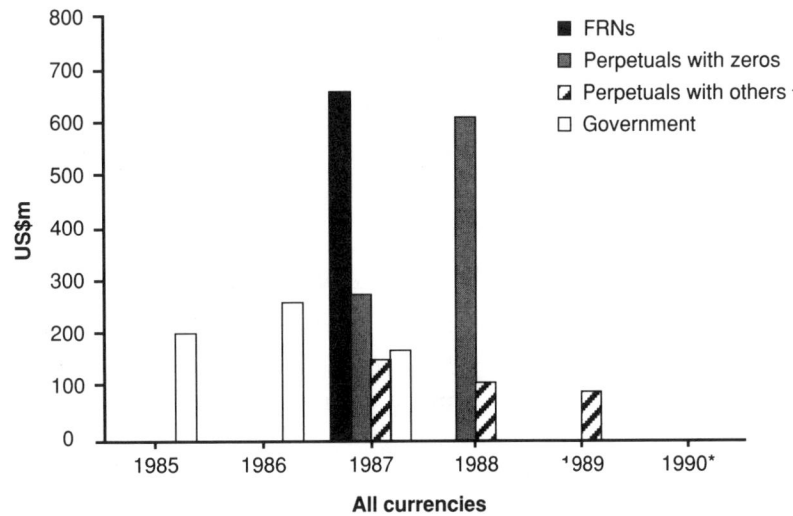

US$m

- FRNs
- Perpetuals with zeros
- Perpetuals with others
- Government

1985 1986 1987 1988 1989 1990*

All currencies

* First three quarters

Source: Euromoney Bondware

Arbitrage opportunities
The differences between the returns on assets and swap rates, which provide arbitrage opportunities, usually occur where assets are especially illiquid or difficult to price. Such assets have to pay abnormally higher yields in order to encourage investors to take the risk that, if interest rates rise or the exchange rate falls (thereby reducing the value of the asset), they would have difficulty finding ready buyers. Typical examples are:

- **Ex-warrant bonds.** These are fixed-income securities issued with attached warrants, which have then been 'stripped' from the bond and sold on. The value of warrants to investors allows these bonds to be issued with low coupons. When warrants are stripped, the price of the so-called 'stub' of the issue goes into deep discount in order to bring the yield on such bonds up to market levels by supplementing the low coupons with capital gains realised when the bond is repaid at face value at maturity. Deeply-discounted bonds tend to be unpopular with investors for a number of reasons (eg, income tax is usually paid on the return represented by the discount as though it accrues like interest, despite the fact that the discount does not yield an actual payment until maturity). The consequent illiquidity of ex-warrant bonds has, in practice, been aggravated by the sheer volume of bonds with warrants which were issued by Japanese borrowers on the back of the equity boom in Japan in the second-half of the 1980s. Swapping relieved the acute oversupply of these bonds which had occurred by 1987 and allowed further dramatic expansion of the warrant market. Ex-warrant bonds have been by far the largest source of assets for swapping.

- **Structured** or **innovative** securities: complex bonds targeted at narrow groups of investors with tailored, often innovative, risk features. These have proved too complex or too narrowly focused and have become illiquid. Classic examples during the 1980s were 'bull' FRNs (on which the rate of return rises if market rates fall) and 'dual currency' bonds (coupons are paid in a currency different to the currency of the redemption principal).

- **Asset-backed** securities, particularly collateralised mortgage obligations (CMOs). These assets tend to offer higher yields than comparable unsecured assets because of the risk of *prepayment* of the underlying assets which will lead to the asset-backed issue being called (when interest rates fall and offer the opportunity for cheaper refinancing). These assets have been swapped using 'putable swaps' — swaps including a put option or right to terminate the swap (putable swaps are described in *Part Three*) — to match the call option represented by the borrowers' rights of prepayment.

- **Illiquid** issues: usually bonds which have been too aggressively priced at issue, weakly syndicated and poorly distributed (a common problem in the Eurobond markets during the 1980s due to competitive pressures); or suffer from the suspect quality of the issuer, the small size of the issue and lack of market-makers. The spread over the relevant benchmark yield on such bonds widens after issue, sometimes dramatically, opening up arbitrage opportunities against swaps. Investors are willing to buy assets swapped from illiquid bonds, because the secondary market problems of the original bonds should be irrelevant to the new asset, if this is priced and structured attractively in its own right.

There are other sources of arbitrage opportunities related to differences in the behaviour of different parts of the capital markets.

- Imbalances between the **supply and demand** for a particular asset. The classic example here was provided by FRNs. As noted already, during the 1980s, commercial banks suffered a shortage of conventional floating interest loan assets to match their floating interest liabilities, as greater use of securities by borrowers eroded their historic customer base and credit demand was curtailed by various lending crises. FRNs provided the substitute. At the same time, the supply of FRNs was interrupted, first, as issuers exercised call options in order to refinance from alternative sources, particularly from the rapidly developing Eurocommercial paper market, and then in 1986, as the collapse of the perpetual FRN market undermined conventional FRNs. Strong bidding for scarce FRNs narrowed margins dramatically. By swapping fixed interest assets to a floating interest basis — to create 'synthetic FRNs' (see the later section 'Types of Asset Swap') — significant arbitrage gains were realised for investors and synthetic FRNs offered considerably more attractive margins than real FRNs. In effect, asset swaps allowed excess demand in the FRN market to be satisfied by supply from the Eurobond market.

- As with liabilities, arbitrage opportunities with assets can arise because of **leads and lags** between the response of different financial markets to the same information. For example, US Treasury securities react rapidly to news, whereas the US dollar Eurobond market is somewhat slower. A rally in US Treasury prices will therefore tend to depress dollar yields and swap rates (which are priced off Treasury yields) in that market in advance of a similar response in Eurobond yields. This opens up the possibility that Eurobonds can be bought at yields high enough relative to swap rates to allow profitable arbitrage into floating interest assets.

- **Swap-driven** issues: some new issues have been priced specifically to swap into floating interest assets (a coupon is paid in excess of swap rates in order to allow arbitrage against asset swaps). This route allowed bond issues by names which are not sufficiently creditworthy to gain ready access to the bond market. Demand for such issues came from commercial banks, for the reasons explained already and because of the traditional willingness of commercial banks (as credit risk intermediaries) to accommodate a wider range of counterparties.

Cross-currency asset swap arbitrage

The examples of arbitrage illustrated so far have involved (single-currency) interest rate swaps. Asset swap arbitrage is also possible with currency swaps. The most common is using *cross-currency* swaps (fixed against floating) to swap from non-dollar fixed interest bonds into floating interest dollars. This type of asset swap is illustrated in Diagram 8:

■ at the start, the investor pays a principal amount of dollars through the swap in exchange for a principal amount of Deutsche marks, which is used to buy Deutsche mark bonds;

■ during the life of the bond, the fixed Deutsche mark interest periodically received on the bond by the investor is paid out through the swap in exchange for floating dollar interest;

■ at maturity, the principal amount of Deutsche marks received by the investor from the repayment of the bond is exchanged through the swap for the original principal amount of dollars: the exchange rate used for the re-exchange of principal amounts is the one agreed at the start of the swap for the original exchange, thus avoiding any currency risk.

Diagram 8: Arbitrage with a cross-currency coupon swap from fixed interest currency to floating interest dollars

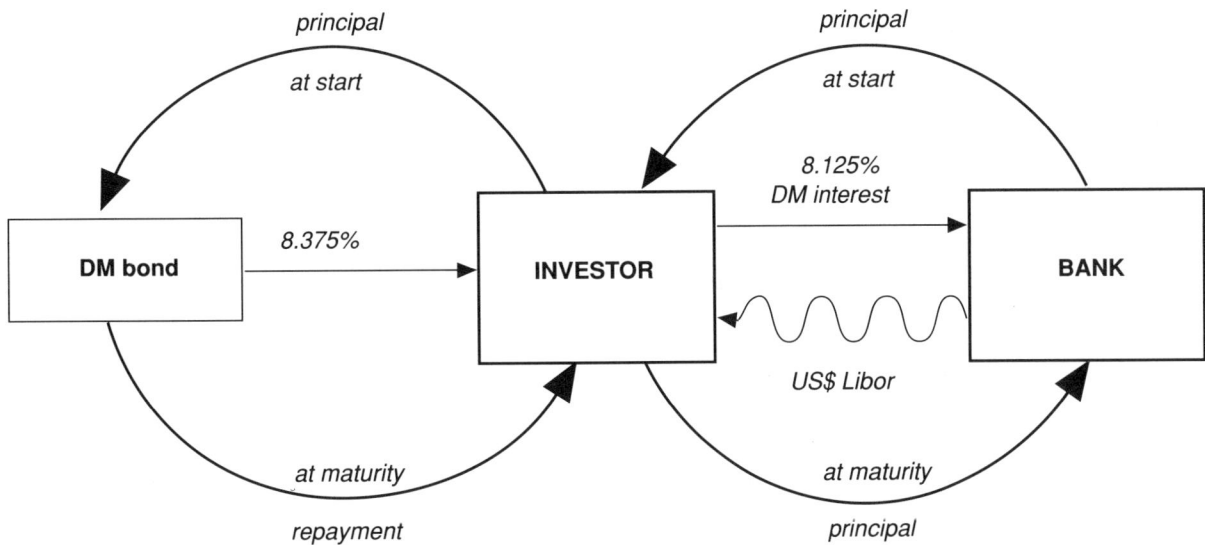

The arbitrage in this asset swap is in the difference between the Deutsche mark interest received on the bond and that paid out through the swap. The arbitrage profit is then added to the floating interest received by the investor. However, the arbitrage profit is in Deutsche marks and the floating interest in dollars. The Deutsche mark profit has to be converted into dollars in the forward foreign exchange market. To calculate the all-in dollar rate of return on the asset swap, the Deutsche mark arbitrage profit can be translated using the **basis conversion factors** published and regularly updated on the IFR Corporate Eye service disseminated on Telerate screen pages 20221–20224 (these are described in the earlier Workbook — *Currency Swaps*).

Receipts	fixed Deutsche mark interest on asset	8.375%pa	arbitrage
	floating dollar interest through swap	Libor	
Payments	fixed Deutsche mark interest through swap	8.125%pa	
Net receipts	floating dollar interest	Libor + 23bp	

Interest is converted using a dollar/Deutsche mark Basis Conversion Factor of 1.100 for dollars to Deutsche marks which is 0.909 for Deutsche marks to dollars.

Cross-currency
arbitrage
opportunities

The discrepancies which provide cross-currency arbitrage opportunities occur for a number of specific reasons, but all have the same effect in encouraging the **segmentation** of the international capital market into distinct currency sectors. As a result of segmentation, the relative pricing of the same two issuers may differ between currency sectors, allowing arbitrage through currency swaps.

- Segmentation limits the **capacity** of particular sectors and means that the supply of new issues by large and frequent borrowers or classes of borrowers can easily saturate demand. A classic example is provided by World Bank issuance in the Swiss franc bond market. Capacity constraints may encourage large issuers to swap into particular currencies rather than issue directly, in order to reduce their cost of funds or to achieve the desired size of funding.

- The segmentation of the international capital market is also apparent in the differences in the **risk premiums** demanded by different currency sectors for lending to one borrower compared to another. For example, the extra margin demanded in the Eurobond and domestic European bond markets for BBB-rated borrowers compared to AAA-rated borrowers has tended to be much less than in the US domestic market. This is the source of the comparative advantage which provides the classic opportunity for new issue arbitrage. The narrower range of risk premiums demanded in some markets reflects a number of factors, including less discriminating credit analysis (which means that some lesser credits get lumped together with better credits), higher savings rates (which produce more abundant capital) and lower absolute yield levels (margins will contract in proportion to overall yields). Traditionally, narrower ranges of risk premiums have been associated with the practice of *name recognition*, which is the subjective preference given to issuers with household names. Name recognition for many years allowed well-known companies like McDonalds to issue cheaper Eurobonds than minor sovereigns like Spain.

- The segmentation of the international capital markets is most obvious where it is imposed in the form of **investment restrictions** such as exchange controls and prudential limits.

- The international capital market is also segmented by a range of subtle **market preferences**, such as an inclination to avoid the inconvenience of settlement or different tax procedures in foreign markets, suspicion towards foreign borrowers and aversion to the currency risk in foreign bonds.

■ Price discrepancies are often generated by **tax** distortions. Where bonds issued in a domestic market are subject to withholding tax on the interest paid, investors may find it difficult or inconvenient to reclaim tax. Such bonds therefore tend to have to offer higher yields to investors in order to offset tax. This type of situation drove the new issue arbitrage which was common between fixed-interest Ecu and floating-interest dollars and is illustrated in Diagram 9. This arbitrage is between Certificati di Credito del Tesoro in Ecu (CTE) issued by the Republic of Italy and AAA-rated Ecu Eurobonds issues. Since September 1986, CTEs have been subject to withholding tax and pay a higher pre-tax yield to compensate investors, at times as much as 100 basis points over good-quality Ecu Eurobonds. Intermediary banks have been able to use this differential to offer Ecu Eurobond issuers a swap into cheap floating-interest dollars and investors an asset swap from CTEs into high-yielding dollar FRNs. In fact, the CTE arbitrage was an important factor behind the development of the Ecu Eurobond market.

Diagram 9: Ecu/dollar new issue tax arbitrage

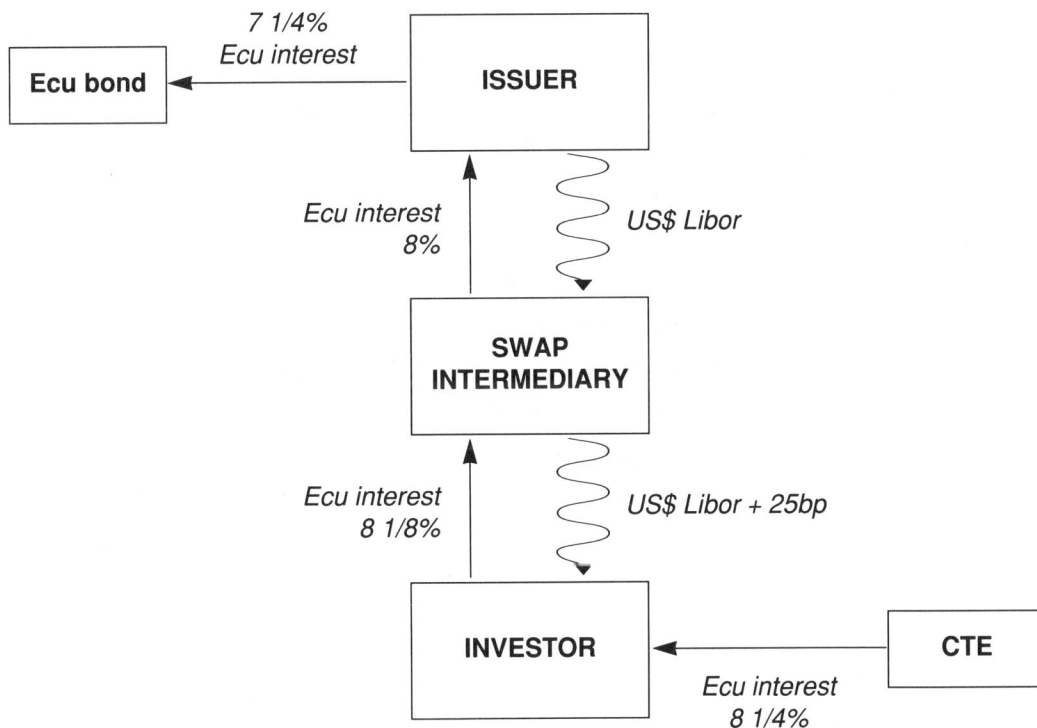

There are a number of points to note about the assets used in swaps:

■   In order to be suitable for swapping, assets must be of good **credit quality,** if the asset swaps are to be sold to investors. Swapping does not resolve credit risk and asset swaps are aimed at investors wanting high-quality assets. Even where asset swaps are being used to provide lesser credits with access to the fixed-income market, the need for credit quality usually requires some form of security, such as a bank guarantee, letter of credit or collateral. It was notable that ex-warrant bonds tended to carry a bank guarantee (this also made them attractive because bank credit risk carries only a 20% risk weight under the Basle Agreement, compared to 100% for corporates).

■   Swapping an asset may be used to shift illiquid securities, but the asset swap will not itself usually be **liquid** in the sense of being actively traded on the secondary market. Indeed, swapping will tend to make liquid securities less liquid. Where illiquid issues are swapped, the aim is generally to structure an asset swap which will appeal to a specific group of new investors. Such customised assets are unlikely to be appropriate for many, if any, other investors. It has been noted that assets swapped into floating interest have typically been sought by commercial banks as substitutes for conventional loan assets, which are not liquid assets, but long-term investments.

■   For the capital market as a whole, arbitrage using asset swaps enhances the **efficiency** of the market by ironing out price discrepancies. Arbitrage effectively puts a floor under prices in both the primary and secondary markets. If a particular issue's price falls and its yield rises far enough to create arbitrage opportunities, demand will emerge for that security to use in swapping.

Types of asset swap

The type of asset swap illustrated so far has the simplest of possible structures, but poses numerous practical problems for investors (see below). In order to overcome these various problems, more complex structures have been developed by swap intermediaries. Unfortunately, the range of asset swap structures has given rise to confusing terminology. Thus, the term 'asset swap' is used both generically, to cover all types of asset swap structure, and specifically to distinguish simpler types of structure from the more complex 'repackaged securities'. The term 'synthetic' is also used to describe the result of any asset swap, yet is also reserved a specific structure. A suggested taxonomy for asset swap structures is set out in Diagram 10.

Diagram 10: Taxonomy of asset swap structures

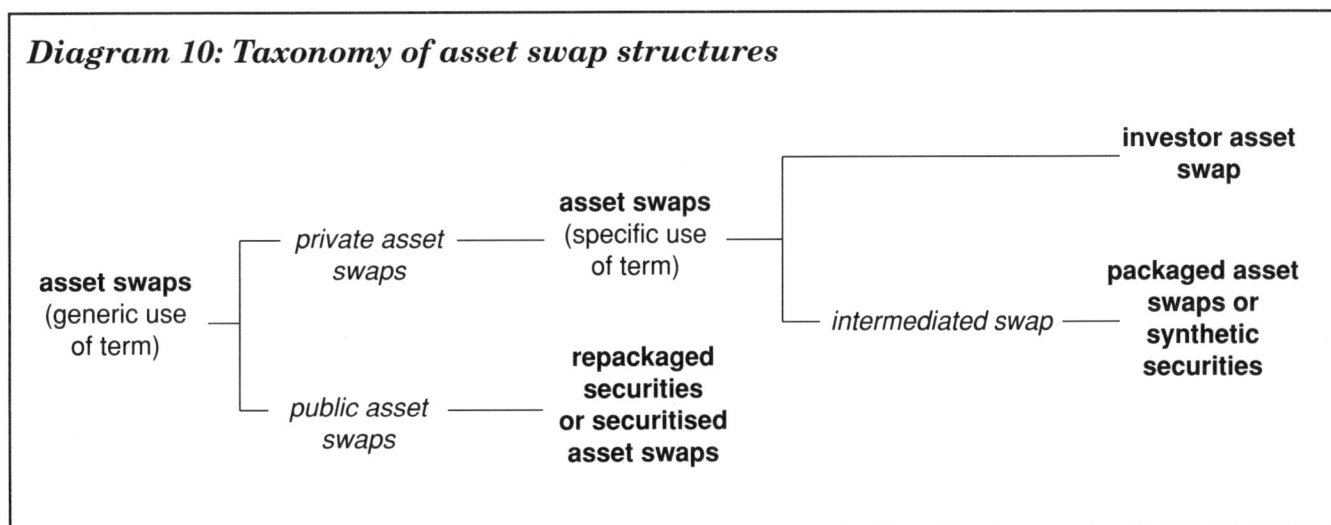

asset swaps (generic use of term)
- *private asset swaps*
  - **asset swaps** (specific use of term)
    - **investor asset swap**
    - *intermediated swap*
      - **packaged asset swaps or synthetic securities**
- *public asset swaps*
  - **repackaged securities or securitised asset swaps**

The difference between 'private' and 'public' asset swaps reflects the fact that, in the first two types of asset swap (investor and packaged), knowledge of the existence of the transaction can be kept entirely to the counterparties. These asset swaps are therefore akin to private placements. Only repackaged securities are publicised, because they involve the issue of a new security (which is why they are also known as 'securitised' asset swaps).

Investor asset swaps

The type of asset swap illustrated so far in *Part Two* — which has the simplest possible transaction structure — is the **investor asset swap**. This involves an investor organising and taking a place at the centre of the structure. An intermediary may propose the asset swap to the investor, sell it the asset and act as its swap counterparty, but it takes no other responsibility.

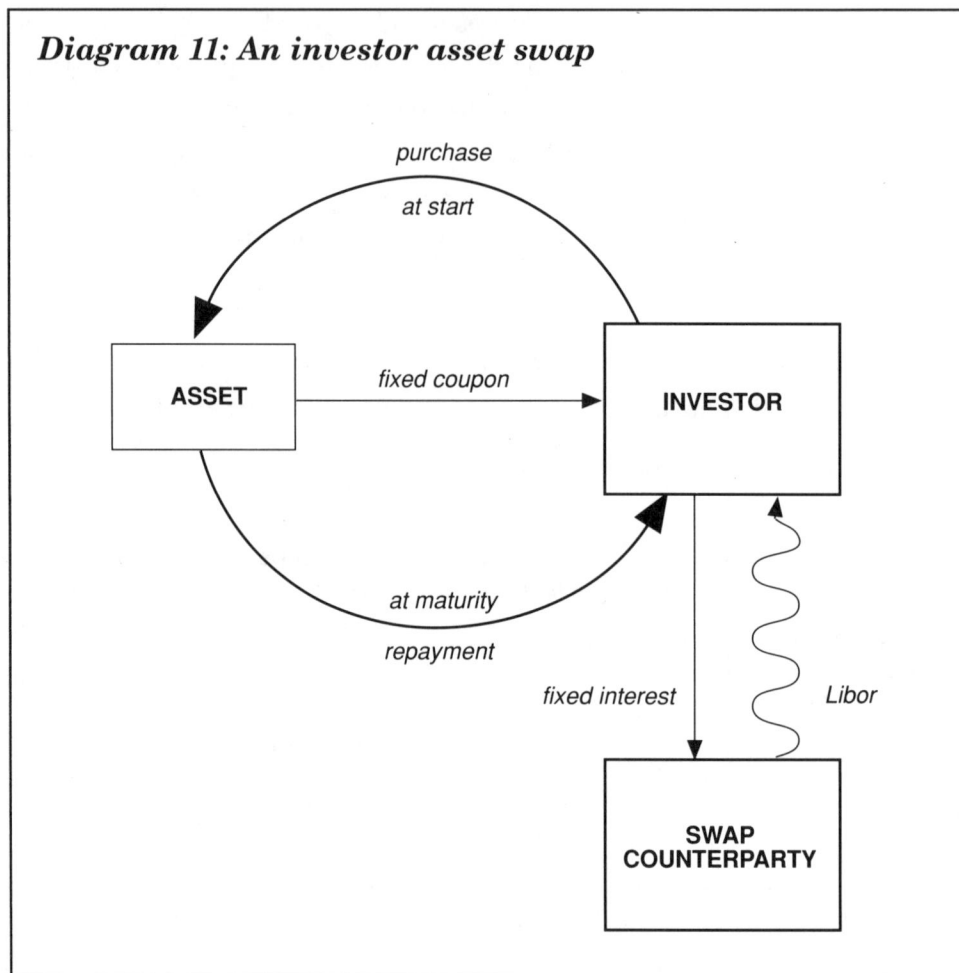

Diagram 11: An investor asset swap

purchase

at start

ASSET → fixed coupon → INVESTOR

at maturity

repayment

fixed interest

Libor

SWAP COUNTERPARTY

As noted already, this structure poses a number of practical problems for the investor:

■ The investor is responsible for the **administration** of the complex set of cash flows.

■   **Accounting** is likely to be complex, possibly requiring separate treatment of the cash asset and the swap, which may distort the perceived benefit of the transaction.

■   The **liquidity** of the asset swap depends on the liquidity of the swap and the asset, and the structure has to be liquidated in two parts, involving two sets of transactions costs.

These drawbacks tend to mean that investor asset swap structures are the preserve of the more sophisticated institutional investor.

Synthetic securities   In order to overcome the problems posed by investor asset swaps, intermediaries usually undertake the organisation of asset swaps on behalf of investors and take their place at the centre of the transactions. The asset being swapped is held by the intermediary for safe-keeping on behalf of the investor and the coupons are legally assigned to the intermediary in order to ensure it of the cash flows for the swap. As the investor only sees the swapped cash flow (not the actual flow from the underlying asset), as far as it is concerned, the asset which it has purchased is producing that cash flow directly. These intermediated asset swaps are therefore called **synthetic securities.** Because this is achieved by the intermediary combining the asset and swap, this structure is also known as a **packaged asset swap**. This type of asset swap structure is by far the most common.

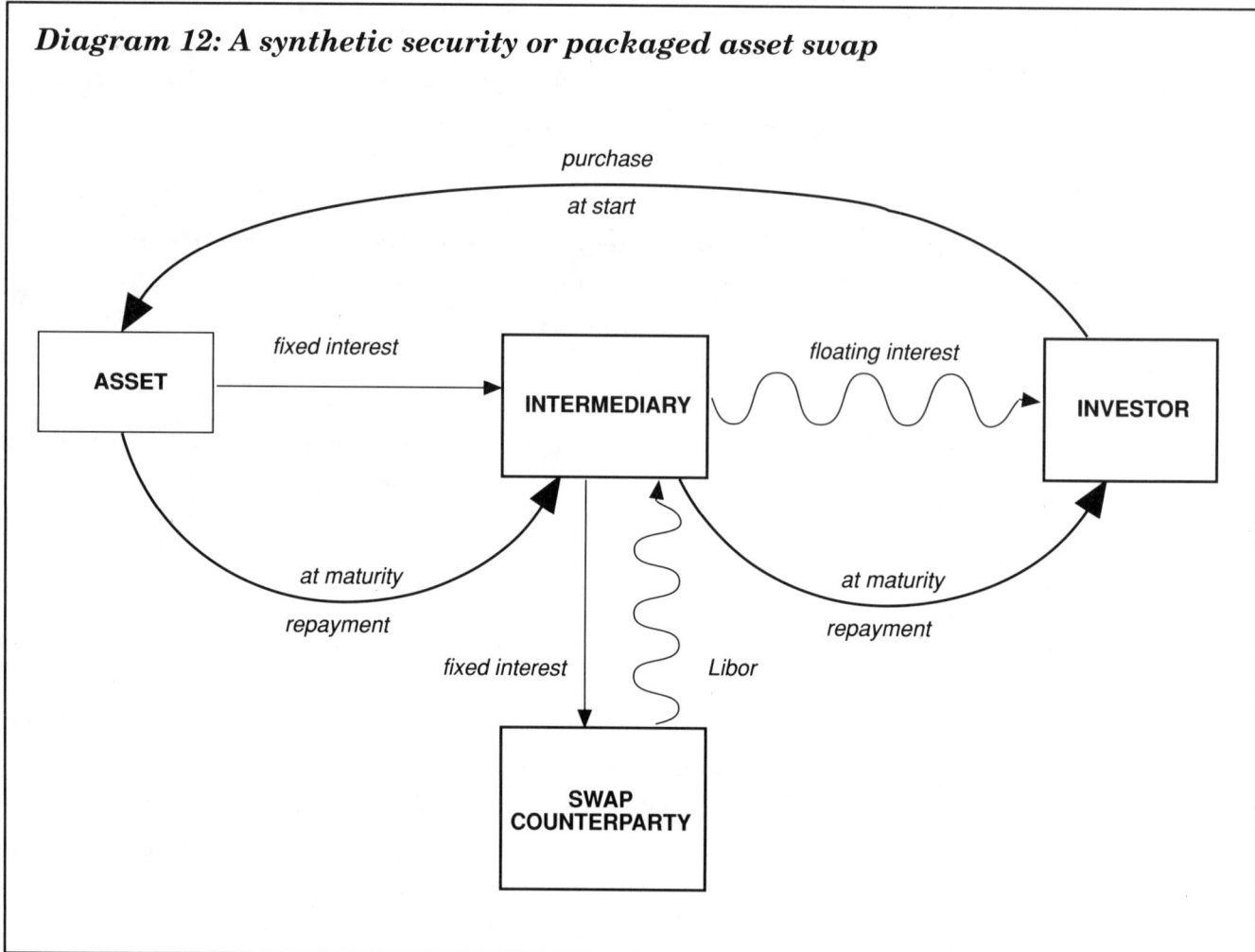

Diagram 12: A synthetic security or packaged asset swap

The advantages of this structure are:

■ the investor sees and is involved in the **administration** of only one cash flow;

■ the **accounting** should be simplified, with the investor able to report the transaction as a single asset;

■ the intermediary can offer **liquidity** to the investor and there should only be a single transactions cost.

Repackaged securities

The attempt represented by packaged asset swaps to simplify asset swap structures for investors and introduce liquidity was taken further in 1985 with the development of repackaged securities. In these asset swaps, investors receive, not just the cash flow, but a negotiable security, for which reason repackaged securities are also known as 'securitised asset swaps'. Repackaged securities are generally created through one-off companies (usually incorporated in an offshore tax haven), called **special purpose vehicles (SPV)**, established to buy and hold an asset and put on a swap (with the intermediary organising the repackaging), and then issue new securities which reflect the characteristics of the swapped asset. The proceeds of the new issue are used to fund the purchase of the assets being swapped and these are used to collateralise the new issue. An asset swap from fixed to floating interest is illustrated in Diagram 13.

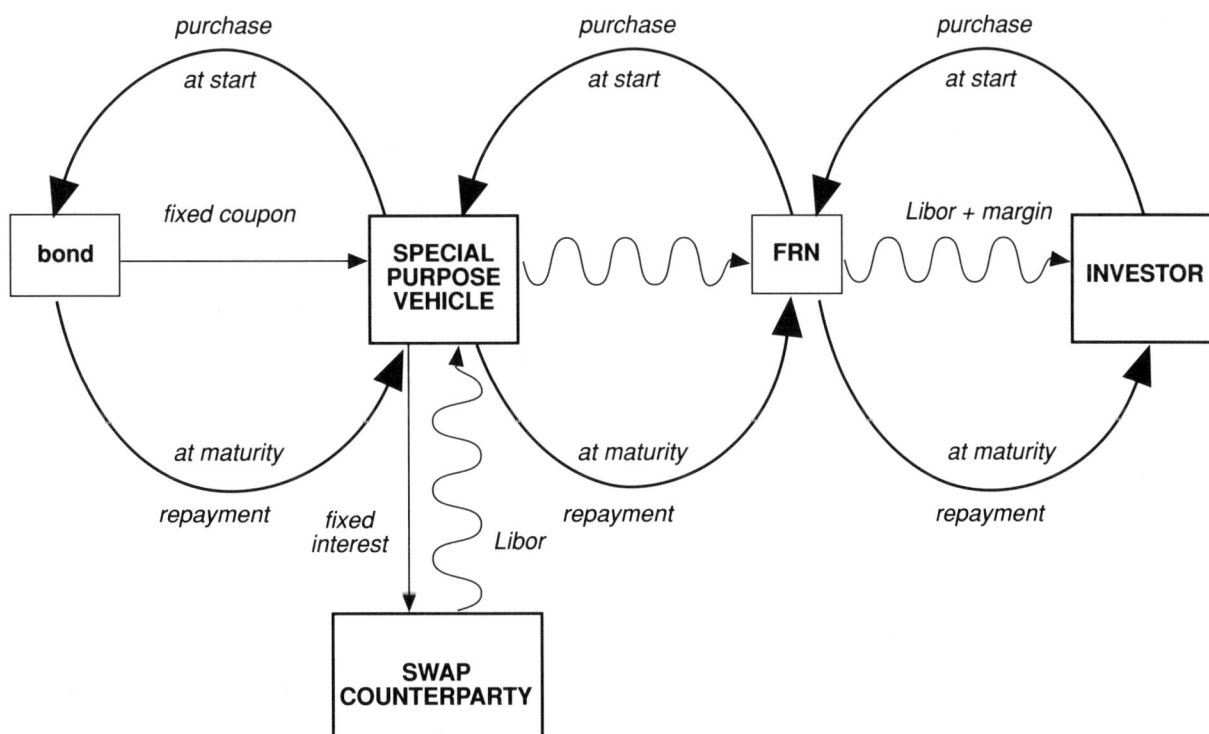

Diagram 13: Repackaged security or securitised asset swap

Because the underlying asset is usually discounted, its face value will be greater than the face value of the repackaged security issued by the SPV. This *overcollateralisation* enhances the credit protection given to the investor.

If the asset to be swapped incorporates special features such as embedded options or sinking funds, these can be passed on by incorporating them in the repackaged security. Alternatively, they can be engineered away, eg, as noted earlier, embedded call options can be hedged with putable swaps and sinking funds by swaps with amortising structures (these types of swap are described in *Part Three*).

A repackaged security is examined in the following case study. This example was one of the very first repackaged securities and involved the swapping of a sovereign issue. Repackaging structures are the means by which ex-warrant bonds are swapped, for which purpose they were first undertaken in 1987. The first cross-currency repackaging was undertaken in 1986. The SPV in this transaction was Banque Paribas Capital Markets' Republic of Italy Euro Repackaged Asset Limited, although the asset swap was more commonly known as 'Ferraris'. It involved the swapping of some Ecu200m of Republic of Italy 1993 Treasury certificates into US dollar floating interest repackaged securities paying Limean.

Case study: A repackaged security

One of the first repackaged securities involved an issue of FRNs by the UK Government in September 1986, an issue which amounted to a record US$4bn and were issued on the finest terms, Libid-1/8%. Morgan Guaranty bought about US$250m of the issue and synthesised fixed-income securities which yielded some 60 basis points over US Treasury notes of the same maturity, despite the AAA-ratings of the UK Government and Morgan (on which there was a credit risk due to the swap)! The FRNs and interest rate swaps were repackaged by using a SPV, Flags BV, to buy and hold the FRNs, transact a coupon swap and then issue some US$250m fixed-income Eurobonds to investors. The proceeds of the new issue funded the purchase of the FRNs and the bonds were collateralised by the FRNs. The transaction is illustrated in Diagram 14 below. It can be seen that Flags BV made a loss of 1/4% per annum by paying Libor through the swap, while only receiving Libid-1/8% on the FRNs, but this was more than offset by the turn of 50 basis points between the fixed interest received through the swap and paid to investors[1].

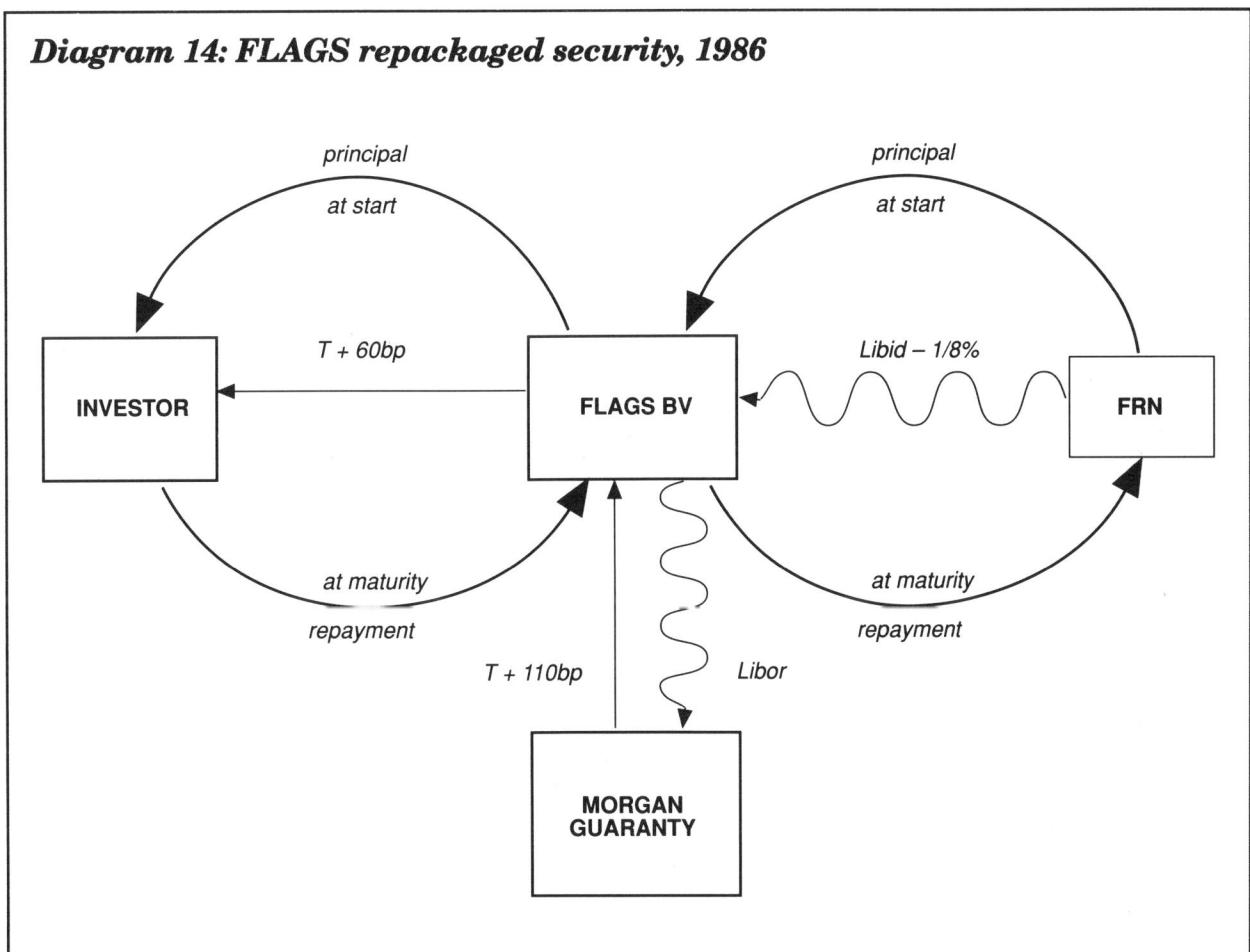

Diagram 14: FLAGS repackaged security, 1986

Notes

1. However, the net gain is not exactly 25bp, as the floating and fixed interest rates are quoted according to different calendar, compounding and coupon payment conventions in this example.

Self-Study Exercises: <u>Questions</u>   Part 2

Question 2.1:   What is the difference between an asset swap and a liability swap?

Question 2.2:   Consider the following asset and swap:

remaining life	= 3 years 201 days
face value	= £100m
clean price	= 102.66 (rounded)
accrued interest	= £4.100m
dirty price	= 106.76 (rounded)
coupon	= 9.125% per annum
current market yield	= 8.20% per annum
coupon payment	= annual
annual basis	= 365 days
swap rate	= 8.20% per annum

Assume an intermediary wishes to swap the asset into a synthetic FRN to sell to an investor, but the investor insists on buying clean assets priced at par.

- Construct the necessary asset swap, using an *investor asset swap* structure.

- Calculate the price of the swap.

Assume the cost of funds to the intermediary is equal to the swap rate.

Question 2.3:   Modify the asset swap in Question 2.2 to eliminate the reinvestment risk to which the investor is exposed.

Question 2.4:   How do asset swaps allow credit risk to be reduced for investors?

Question 2.5:   Describe six typical arbitrage opportunities for asset swaps

Question 2.6:   How, if at all, do asset swaps change the liquidity and credit risk of the assets being swapped?

Question 2.7:   What is the difference between *private* and *public* asset swap structures?

Question 2.8:   What are the drawbacks to *investor asset swaps*? How are these drawbacks overcome by the packaged asset swap structure?

Question 2.9:   What advantages do *repackaged securities* provide over other types of asset swap structure?

Question 2.10:   Draw a typical *repackaged asset swap* from a floating to fixed interest basis.

Self-Study Exercises: <u>Answers</u>   Part 2

Answer 2.1:
- ■ An asset swap is linked to an asset; a liability swap is linked to a liability.

  (1/2 mark)

- ■ Asset swaps are used by investors; liability swaps are used by borrowers.

  (1/2 mark)

- ■ Cash flows come from the asset into the swap in an asset swap; they go out of the swap to the liability in a liability swap.

  (1/2 mark)

- ■ However, the structure of the swap mechanism in an asset swap is no different to that in a liability swap.

  (1/2 mark)

  (Total marks = 2)

Answer 2.2:   The asset swap is illustrated in the diagram:

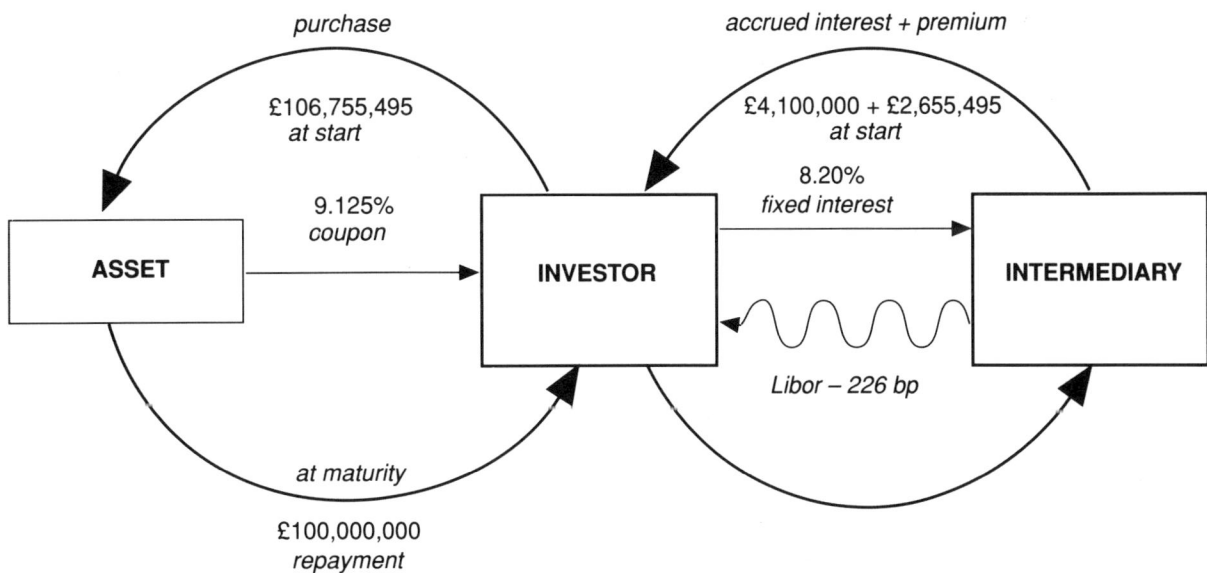

As shown in the diagram, the asset swap involves the following steps:

■ The investor buys an amount of the asset with a face value of £100,000,000 for a dirty price of £106,757,928: consisting of the clean price of £102,657,928 plus accrued interest of:

£100,000,000 x 12.5/100 x 90/365 = £4,100,000

(1 mark)

■ The investor puts on a coupon swap with a notional principal amount of £100,000,000 in which it pays fixed interest.

(1 mark)

■ The swap intermediary compensates the investor for the accrued interest which the latter has paid as part of the dirty price of the asset (£4,100,000), with an equivalent upfront cash payment. In effect, therefore, the investor ends up buying a clean asset.

(1 mark)

■ The intermediary recoups this early payment of interest (the investor would otherwise have to wait until the next coupon date — which is 201 days after purchasing the asset — before receiving this interest), and the cost of funding it for 201 days, by subtracting a margin from the Libor paid to the investor through the swap. The margin needed to recoup the £4,100,000 at the assumed funding rate of 8.20% per annum is calculated by amortising £4,100,000 over the remaining life of the asset (3 years and 201 days):

n   = 3.551 years (3 years 201 days)
PV = −4.100000
FV = 0
i   = 8.20%

which gives:

PMT = 1.374%

(2 marks)

■ The intermediary offsets the premium which the investor has paid for the asset — and the corresponding excess of the coupon rate (9.125%) over the current market rate (8.20%) — by making an upfront cash payment to the investor equal to the premium (£2,655,495).

(1 mark)

■ The intermediary is recompensed for the upfront cash payment it makes to the investor by subtracting a margin from the Libor which the intermediary pays to the investor through the swap. Assuming a cost of funding of 8.20% per annum, this margin is calculated by amortising the amount of the premium over the remaining life of the asset (3 years and 201 days):

n   = 3.551 years (3 years 201 days)
PV = −2.655495
FV = 0
i   = 8.20%

which gives a margin of:

PMT = 0.890%

(2 marks)

■ The total margin below the Libor received by the investor through the swap is therefore:

accrued interest	−1.374%
premium	−0.890%
margins +/ Libor	2.264%

(1 mark)

(Total marks = 9)

Answer 2.3: The reinvestment risk to which the investor is exposed through the asset swap in the previous question is due to the mismatch between the coupon rate and the swap rate. It is eliminated by putting on a *premium swap* which pays the coupon rate of 9.125% per annum, rather than the current swap rate of 8.20%. However, the intermediary compensates the investor for the extra interest payments by either:

(1 mark)

- making an upfront *cash payment* to the investor equal to the difference in interest paid by the investor through the swap at 9.125% per annum compared to 8.20% per annum discounted back to present value:

Period after purchase of asset (years)	Fixed interest payments through swap at:		Differential (A) – (B)	Present value of differential
	Current swap rate of 8.20% pa (A)	Off-market swap rate of 9.125% pa (B)		
0.551	4,515,616	9,125,000	–4,609,384	–4,413,615
1.551	8,200,000	9,125,000	–925,000	–818,589
2.551	8,200,000	9,125,000	–925,000	–756,552
3.551	8,200,000	9,125,000	–925,000	–699,216
	Net present value of differential in interest streams			–6,687,972

It is important to note here that the most significant change in fixed interest payments through the swap occurs at the first payment date, when a payment for a full interest period is paid through the swap — in order to match the full coupon received by the investor on the asset.

(5 marks)

- adding a margin to the Libor paid to the investor through the swap which is equal to the net present value of £6,687,972 over the remaining life of the asset (3 years and 201 days):

```
n    = 3.551 years (3 years 201 days)
PV   = −6.687972
FV   = 0
i    = 8.20%
```

gives:

PMT = 2.241%

(2 marks)

■ If the adjustment for the premium swap is made in the form of a margin against Libor, rather than an upfront cash payment, the total margin against the Libor received by the investor through the swap would be:

```
accrued interest   −1.374%
premium            −0.890%
premium swap       +2.241%

margins +/− Libor  −0.023%
```

(1 mark)

(Total marks = 9)

Answer 2.4: Asset swaps can reduce credit risk to the investor by:

■ facilitating *diversification* of portfolios by expanding the range of assets available for investment: for investors who prefer to invest only in familiar markets, asset swaps can introduce assets issued by borrowers who only issue in other markets, by swapping assets from those other markets.

(1 mark)

■ *asset-backing*: repackaged securities offer investors reduced credit risk, as they are collateralised with other (high-quality) assets.

(1 mark)

(Total marks = 2)

Answer 2.5: Arbitrage opportunities arise when the interest rates on assets diverge from comparable swap rates, usually when assets pay higher yields. Several examples have been described in this Workbook:

- **Ex-warrant** bonds. Stripped of their warrants, these low-coupon bonds go into deep discount in order to bring their yields up to current market levels. As deeply-discounted bonds tend to be unpopular with investors, the yields tend to be above normal.

- **Structured** or **innovative** securities. These are complex bonds with tailored, often innovative, risk features which are targeted at narrow groups of investors. The complexity or customisation of such bonds often makes them illiquid and they pay an illiquidity premium in their yield.

- **Asset-backed** securities such as CMOs. These assets tend to offer higher yields than comparable unsecured assets because of the risk of *prepayment* of the underlying assets, which will lead to the asset-backed issue being called before maturity.

- **Illiquid** issues. These are usually bonds which have been too aggressively priced at issue, weakly syndicated and poorly distributed; or suffer from the suspect quality of the issuer, the small size of the issue and lack of market-makers. The spread over the relevant benchmark yield on such bonds widens after issue, sometimes dramatically.

- When imbalances occur between the **supply and demand** for a particular asset. The classic example here was in the FRN market. There was strong demand for FRNs from commercial banks in the second-half of the 1980s due to a shortage of conventional floating interest loan assets. At the same time, the supply of FRNs was interrupted repeatedly. Margins over Libor narrowed dramatically. By swapping bonds to create synthetic FRNs significant arbitrage gains were realised.

- Arbitrage opportunities can arise because of **leads and lags** between the response of different financial markets to the same information. For example, US Treasury securities react rapidly to news, whereas the US dollar Eurobond market is somewhat slower. A rally in US Treasury prices will Treasury yields and dollar swap rates (which are priced off Treasury yields) in advance of a similar response in Eurobond yields. This opens up the possibility that Eurobonds can be bought at yields high enough relative to swap rates to allow profitable arbitrage by swapping into floating interest assets.

■ **Swap-driven** issues: some new issues have been priced specifically to swap into floating interest assets. This route has allowed bond issues by names which are not sufficiently creditworthy to gain ready access to the bond market, but are able to raise floating interest funds and are willing to end up paying a higher coupon on the fixed interest funds into which they are swapping in order to gain effective access to the bond market.

■ The limited **capacity** of particular currency sectors of the capital market means that the supply of new issues by large and frequent borrowers can easily saturate demand and drive up the yields demanded by investors. This opens the way for new issue arbitrage with borrowers who rarely issue in the same sector and who are able to pay lower yields because of their scarcity value.

■ Differences in the **risk premiums** demanded by different currency sectors for lending to one borrower compared to another. For example, the margin between the yields demanded in the Eurobond and domestic European bond markets for BBB-rated borrowers compared to AAA-rated borrowers has tended to be much less than in the US domestic market. This is the classic new issue arbitrage opportunity.

■ Where **investment restrictions** are imposed, investors may be willing to pay higher yields to acquire otherwise inaccessible assets made available indirectly through asset swaps.

■ Price discrepancies generated by **tax** distortions. Where bonds issued in a domestic market are subject to withholding tax on the interest paid, investors may find it difficult or inconvenient to reclaim tax. Such bonds therefore tend to have to offer higher yields to investors in order to offset tax.

(Total marks = 6)

Answer 2.6:

■ Although the swapping of an asset may be used to shift illiquid securities from portfolios, swapped assets do not tend to be any more liquid themselves. This is because asset swaps are generally customised to appeal to a specific group of new investors.

(1 mark)

■ Swapping cannot reduce the credit risk on individual assets (although it can reduce the overall credit risk in portfolios by facilitating diversification — see Answer 2.4). Asset swaps can be used to provide lesser credits with effective access to the bond market (because these lesser names can issue in the more relaxed floating interest market, they can be swapped into fixed interest). However, such asset swaps are usually reinforced by some form of security, such as a bank guarantee, letter of credit or collateral.

(1 mark)

(Total marks = 2)

Answer 2.7:

■ Investor and packaged asset swaps are called *private* because all the necessary transactions are bilateral, which allows knowledge of the existence of these transaction to be kept entirely among the counterparties.

(1 mark)

■ Repackaged securities are called *public,* because they involve the issue of new securities which are marketed openly to investors.

(1 mark)

(Total marks = 2)

Answer 2.8:

Investor asset swaps pose a number of practical problems for the investor:

■ The investor is responsible for the **administration** of the complex set of cash flows.

(1/2 mark)

- **Accounting** is likely to be complex, possibly requiring separate treatment of the asset and the swap, which may distort the perceived benefit of the transaction.

(1/2 mark)

- The **liquidity** of the asset swap depends on the liquidity of the swap and the asset, and the structure has to be liquidated in two parts, involving two sets of transactions costs.

(1/2 mark)

In *packaged asset swaps*, intermediaries usually undertake the organisation of asset swaps on behalf of investors and take their place at the centre of the transactions. This type of structure overcomes the problems associated with investor asset swaps:

- The investor sees and is involved in the **administration** of only one cash flow;

(1/2 mark)

- The **accounting** should be simplified, with the investor able to report the transaction as a single asset;

(1/2 mark)

- The intermediary can offer **liquidity** to the investor and there should only be a single transactions cost.

(1/2 mark)

(Total marks = 3)

Answer 2.9:   *Repackaged securities* offer several improvements on the packaged asset swap, by:

- adding **liquidity** to asset swaps in the form of the repackaged security;

(1 mark)

- reducing the **credit risk** to the investor by overcollateralisation (because the underlying asset is usually discounted, its face value will be greater than the face value of the repackaged security).

(1 mark)

(Total marks = 2)

Answer 2.10:

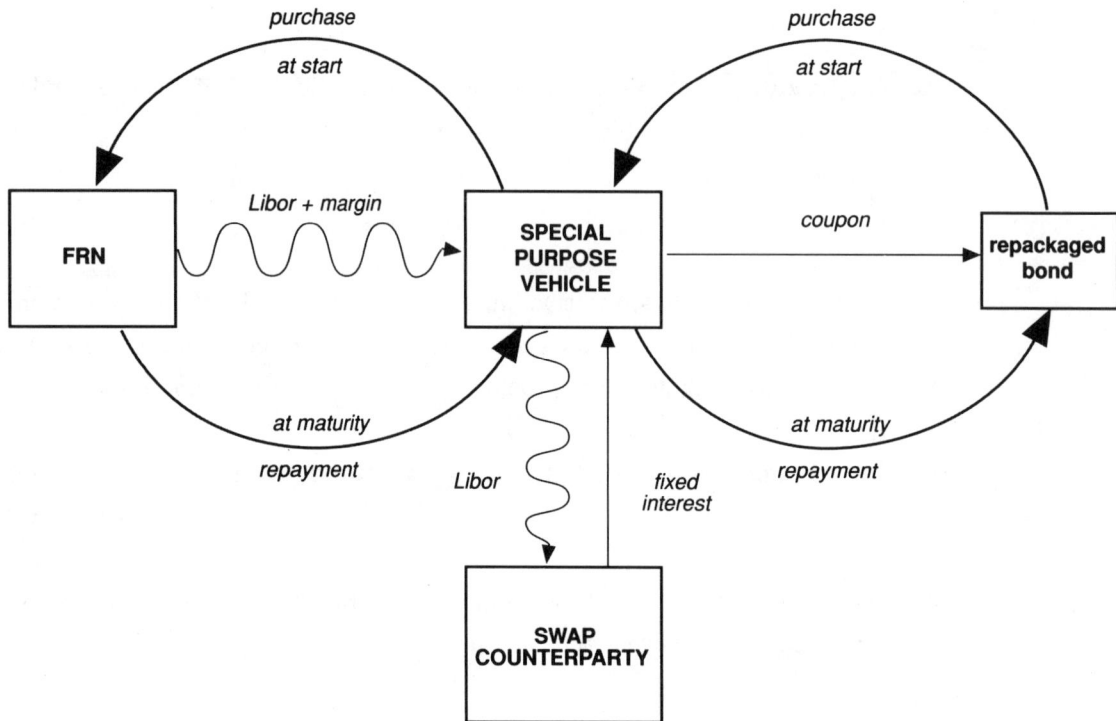

(Total marks = 3)

3 Non-generic swaps

What are generic and non-generic swaps?

Definition	A generic swap is an interest rate or currency swap which has the simplest structure possible. Specifically, a generic swap has — and a non-generic swap does not — all of the following characteristics: ■ constant principal amount (notional principal amounts in interest rate swaps and actual principal amounts in currency swaps); ■ an exchange of fixed for floating interest or — in the case of some currency swaps — fixed for fixed interest: ■ any fixed rate of interest is constant; ■ any floating rate of interest is 'flat' — in other words, there is no margin over the floating-rate index; ■ payments of interest (fixed or floating) are made regularly; ■ interest starts accruing no later than for 'spot' value (ie, two business days after the transaction is agreed); ■ no special risk features (eg, attached options)

Alternative names for generic and non-generic swaps

As with other financial instruments, generic versions of swaps are also known as **straight** or **plain vanilla** swaps. Non-generic swaps are sometimes referred to as **exotic** swaps.

The relationship between generic and non-generic swaps

All non-generic swaps can be synthesised with generic swaps, which means it is possible to *hedge* the risk on a non-generic swap with generic swaps.

While a non-generic swap is still new, there will usually be a significant difference between the price at which the non-generic swap can be transacted and the price of a hedge constructed from generic swaps. This reflects the fact that only a few swap intermediaries will initially understand how to hedge new non-generic swaps. In such circumstances, the price of a non-generic swap will be set in response to supply and demand, rather than the cost of hedging it. Swap intermediaries willing to transact a new type of non-generic swap — because they know how to hedge the risk on it or because they are willing to take the uncovered risk — will be able to profit from the differences between the price at which the non-generic swap can be transacted and the price of the hedge constructed from generic swaps. Such differences are what is meant by *arbitrage* opportunities.

Generally, intermediaries willing to transact a new type of non-generic swap will have devised an innovative method of hedging the risk on it (using generic swaps). While this method of hedging remains proprietary to a limited number of intermediaries, they can profit from arbitrage opportunities. Eventually, the non-generic swap and methods of hedging it will become more widely understood. More intermediaries will then offer it to customers and increasing competition will force intermediaries to sacrifice arbitrage opportunities.

If transactions in a non-generic swap become sufficiently common and a market with some liquidity begins to develop, swap intermediaries may be able to hedge directly between non-generic swaps of the same type, rather than against generic swaps.

What do non-generic swaps do?

Non-generic swaps are usually designed to manage the risk or exploit arbitrage opportunities in complex underlying transactions. The need to apply swaps to complex situations reflects:

- the growing use of swaps as an instrument of *asset and liability management* — including not only the management of interest rate and currency risk, but also the engineering of cash flows for liquidity purposes;

- the need to keep innovating in order to develop new *arbitrage* opportunities as old ones are exhausted by competition.

Non-generic structures exist in both interest rate and currency swaps: for simplicity, however, this Workbook mainly uses interest rate swaps as examples. There are also non-generic asset and liability swaps, but the structure of the swap remains the same in both cases.

Types of non-generic swap

Classifying non-generic swaps

Given that a generic swap is defined in terms of the seven characteristics listed above, it follows that non-generic swaps can be classified in terms of variations which are made to any of these characteristics. A taxonomy of non-generic swaps organised along these lines is set out in Table 4.

Alternatively, non-generic swaps can be grouped according to how they are synthesised and thereby hedged from generic swaps. Some are synthesised by combining several generic swaps; others through combination with other types of risk management instrument, such as futures and options. This chapter divides non-generic swaps into two groups on this basis:

■   **composite** non-generic swaps — combinations of several generic swaps:

amortising swaps
accreting swaps
roller-coaster swaps
basis swaps
step-up/step-down swaps
spreadlock swaps
swaps with margins over floating index
deferred-coupon swaps
deferred-coupon FRN swaps
premium/discount swaps
zero-coupon swaps
delayed-start swaps
forward swaps

■   swap **derivatives** — combinations of generic swaps and other types of risk management instrument:

swap futures
options on swaps

Table 4: Basic taxonomy of non-generic swaps

Generic swap characteristics	Non-generic variation of swap characteristics	Name of non-generic swap
Constant (notional or actual) principal amount	principal amount decreases	amortising swap
	principal amount increases	accreting swap
	principal amount increases, then decreases	roller-coaster swap
Fixed against floating or fixed interest	floating against floating interest	basis swap
Constant fixed rate of interest	fixed rate increases or decreases in stages	step-up/step-down swap
	swap spread fixed in advance of benchmark yield	spreadlock swap
Flat floating interest rate	margin over floating interest rate index	
Regular payment of interest	fixed interest payments deferred	deferred-coupon swap
	floating interest payments deferred	deferred-coupon FRN swap
	fixed interest payments all deferred to maturity	zero-coupon swap
	fixed interest payments advanced or deferred as cash payment	premium/discount swap
Immediate or 'spot' start	late start	delayed-start swap
		forward swap
No special risk features	future on swap	swap futures
	option on swap	swaption
		callable/putable swap
		extendible swap
		contingent swap
	future and option	options on swap futures

Composite non-generic swaps

Swaps with variable principal amounts

Types and uses of swaps with variable principal amounts

There are three basic types of interest rate swaps with principal amounts — notional in interest rate swaps and actual in currency swaps — that vary over the life of the swap:

■ **amortising** swaps;

■ **accreting** swaps;

■ **roller-coaster** swaps.

Amortising swap

Amortising swaps have principal amounts which *decrease* in steps over the life of the swap. They are used in conjunction with instruments with amortising (non-bullet) redemption structures — eg, bond issues with sinking or purchase funds — lease transactions with periodic mixed principal and interest rental payments and mortgage-backed securities with expected prepayment schedules.

Accreting swap

Accreting swaps have principal amounts which *increase* in steps over the life of the swap. They are used in conjunction with instruments with some form of periodic drawdown or take-up — eg, project financing facilities.

Roller-coaster swap

Roller-coaster swaps are a combination of an amortising and accreting swap: the principal amount increases in steps and then decreases in steps. Applications include project financing facilities with periodic drawdown, followed by an amortised repayment.

Non-generic swaps

Constructing swaps with variable principal amounts

Swaps with variable principal amounts are usually quite simple to construct, as they can be broken down into a series of generic swaps.

Amortising swap

An amortising swap is simply a series of generic swaps with increasing maturities. A basic amortising swap structure is analysed in Diagram 15.

Diagram 15: Constructing an amortising swap

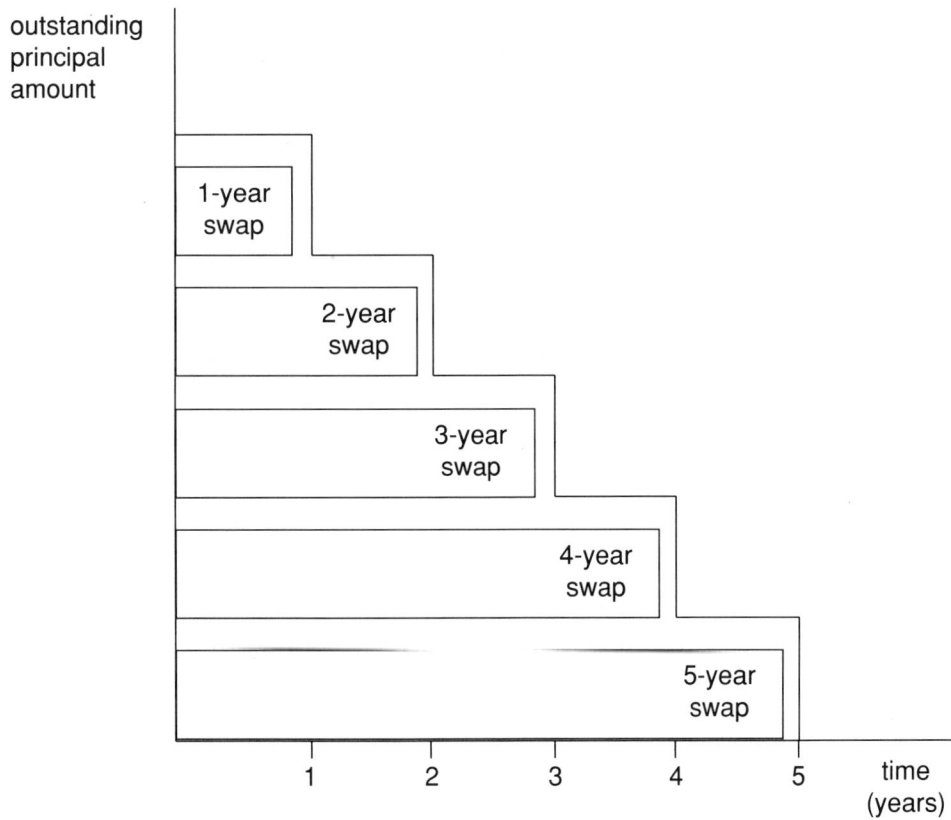

Accreting swap

An accreting swap is a series of one generic swap (which has a spot start) and several delayed-start swaps (which are described below) with increasingly-delayed dates. A simple accreting swap structure is analysed in Diagram 16.

Diagram 16: Constructing an accreting swap

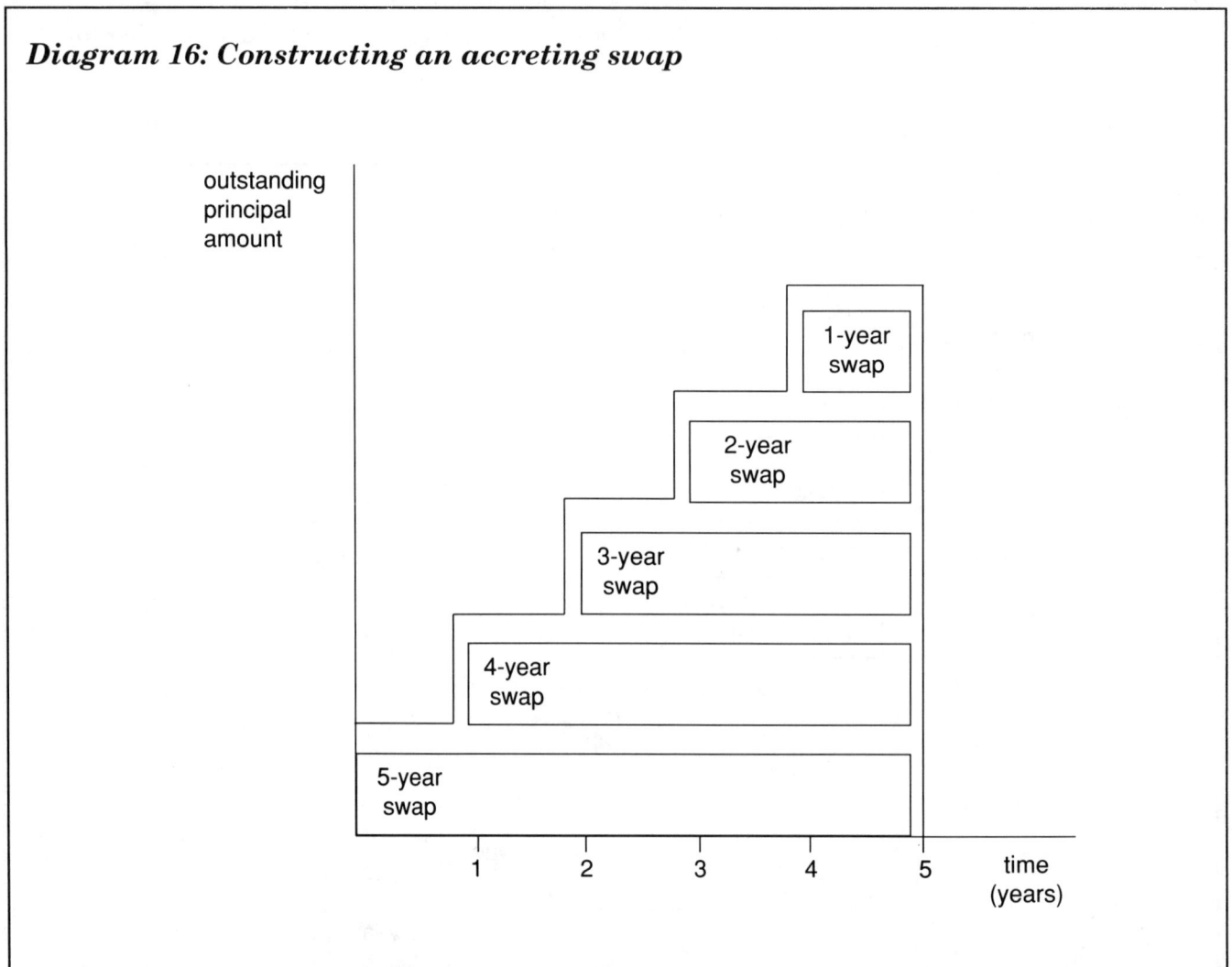

outstanding
principal
amount

1-year
swap

2-year
swap

3-year
swap

4-year
swap

5-year
swap

| 1 | 2 | 3 | 4 | 5 | time (years) |

Roller-coaster swap   As will probably be apparent, a roller-coaster swap is effectively just a combination of an amortising and an accreting swap.

Diagram 17: Constructing a roller-coaster swap

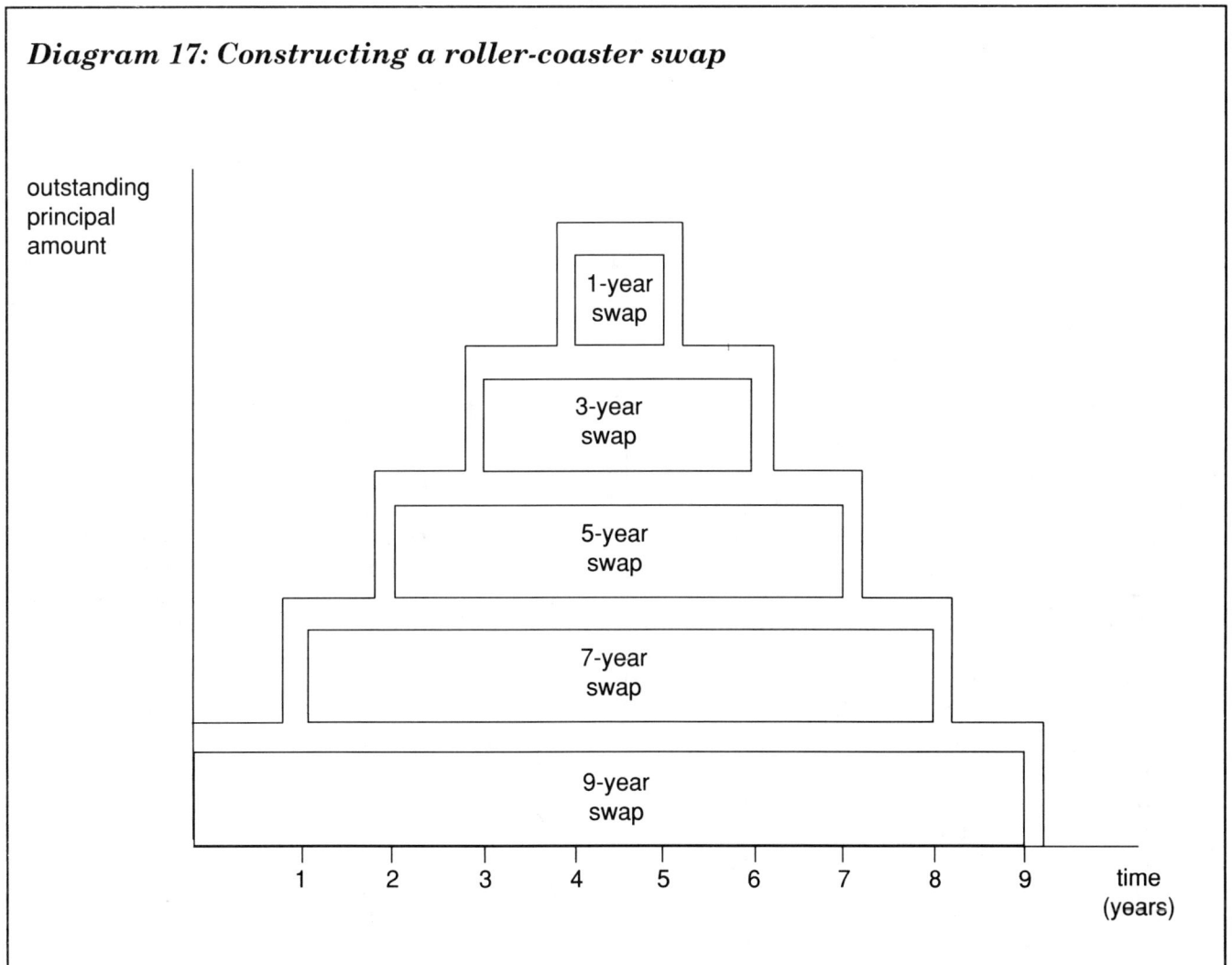

Pricing swaps with variable principal amounts

Given that a swap with a variable principal amount can be broken down into a series of generic swaps, the price of such a swap is a weighted average of the prices of the generic swaps into which it can be decomposed, with the price of each generic swap weighted by its principal amount and tenor. The prices of the generic swaps should be readily available in liquid swap markets. A risk premium may be added to the calculated average swap price to reflect the frequency or irregularity of the change in principal amount.

An example

The pricing of an amortising swap is illustrated in Table 5.

Table 5: Pricing an amortising swap

Tenor (years)	Principal amount of amortising swap (million)	Principal amount of generic swap (million)	Generic swap price (%pa)	Principal amount of generic swap weighted by tenor (million)	Principal amount of generic swap weighted by tenor and swap price (million)
Spot	100				
0.5	90	10	8.05	5	0.403
1.0	80	10	8.15	10	0.815
1.5	70	10	8.30	15	1.245
2.0	60	10	8.32	20	1.664
2.5	50	10	8.35	25	2.088
3.0	40	10	8.48	30	2.544
3.5	30	10	8.66	35	3.031
4.0	20	10	8.87	40	3.548
4.5	10	10	8.95	45	4.028
5.0	0	10	9.03	50	4.515
sub-totals				275 [A]	23.881 [B]
Weighted average swap rate (= [B] / [A] x 100)					**8.68%pa**

Basis swaps

A basis swap — sometimes called an 'index' swap — is an exchange of two streams of interest payments which are calculated using different floating interest rate indexes. The concept is illustrated in Diagram 18.

Diagram 18: Basis swap

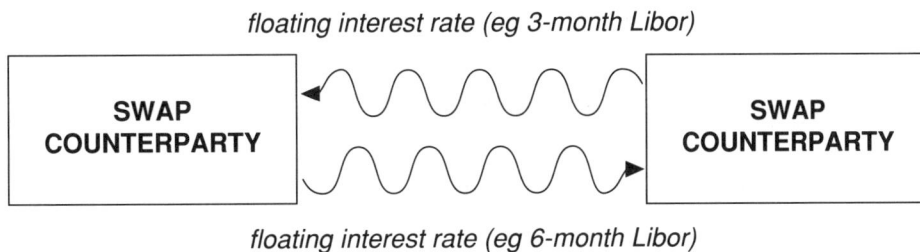

floating interest rate (eg 3-month Libor)

SWAP COUNTERPARTY

SWAP COUNTERPARTY

floating interest rate (eg 6-month Libor)

Types of basis swap

Basis swaps can be between a variety of floating interest rate indexes:

- *different tenors* of the same index, eg, three-month Libor against six-month Libor;

- the same or different tenors of *different indexes*, eg, three-month US dollar Libor against three-month US Treasury bill yield or six-month US dollar Libor against US Prime Rate;

- an index and its *average*, eg, six-month Libor against the weekly average of six-month Libor over six months.

Most basis swaps are against Libor. US dollar basis swaps will typically exchange US dollar Libor against any one of a number of floating interest rate indexes:

■ US Prime Rate

■ Federal Reserve *Commercial Paper Composite Index* (the 'H-15' Index)[1]

■ US Treasury bill yield

■ yield on bankers' acceptances

■ yield on certificates of deposit

■ Federal Funds rate

■ *Kenny Index* [2]

■ *Cost of Funds Indexes* for Federal Home Loan Banks (S & L associations)

Most activity in US dollar basis swaps is between Libor on the one hand and Prime Rate, US CP yields and US Treasury bill (T-bills) yields. The importance of the Treasury bill yield reflects the requirement of US Federal Agencies for funding linked to this rate. In the UK, basis swaps are typically between sterling Libor and building societies' mortgage rates.

Given the role of Libor as a benchmark, the price of basis swaps is usually quoted as margins above or below the non-Libor index being swapped (the other side of the swap being Libor). Table 6 sets out illustrative prices for basis swaps between US dollar Libor on the one hand and yields on US CP, US Treasury bills and US Prime Rate. From this table, it can be seen that a two-year CP/Libor basis swap is quoted as '29/33', which means the quoting bank is willing to transact swaps in which it either:

■ pays 29 basis points above the current yield on US CP in return for receiving Libor flat;

■ receives 33 basis points above the current yield on US CP in return for paying Libor flat.

For a two-year Prime/Libor basis swap, the quote is '–126/–123': the quoting bank is willing to transact swaps in which it either:

■ pays 126 basis points below the current US Prime Rate in return for receiving Libor flat;

■ receives 123 basis points below the current US Prime Rate in return for paying Libor flat.

Table 6: Basis swap prices

Term	CP/Libor	T-bill/Libor	Prime/Libor
2 years	29/33	128/135	–126/–123
3 years	29/32	132/138	–131/–126
4 years	30/35	124/129	–131/–126
5 years	31/36	132/137	–132/–126

Uses of basis swaps

Basis swaps have a number of typical uses:

■ To *hedge* basis risk, meaning a mismatch between two floating interest rates. The first basis swaps were exchanges of US Prime Rate and US dollar Libor designed to hedge the basis risk which faced European banks — which funded themselves at Libor — when sovereign syndicated loans in which they were participating were rescheduled and repriced at US Prime Rate. Where basis swaps are not available against overnight interest rates, the basis risk between overnight and term interest rates — eg, where a six-month asset is funded by overnight borrowing — can be partially hedged with basis swaps between an index and its average, eg, six-month Libor against the weekly average of six-month Libor over six months, so-called **reset swaps**. The fact that the calculation of the average involves the more frequent refixing of Libor means it behaves like a very short-term rate and should change almost in step with the overnight rate.

■ To *synthesise* funding in an inaccessible or inconvenient market, eg, non-US borrowers swapping from Libor into US CP rates without having to obtain credit ratings.

■ To *arbitrage* the floating interest rate indexes which can be received through basis swaps against the actual cost of funds to an individual borrower, eg the H-15 CP index used in basis swaps might be higher than the actual cost of funds to a prime company with a well-established US CP programme, allowing it to arbitrage between the two and reduce its all-in cost of funds in terms of, say, Libor. This arbitrage is illustrated in Diagram 19. In effect, the borrower is using its funding power in one market to reduce its cost of funds in terms of another interest rate better suited to its asset and liability management.

Diagram 19: Arbitrage with a basis swap

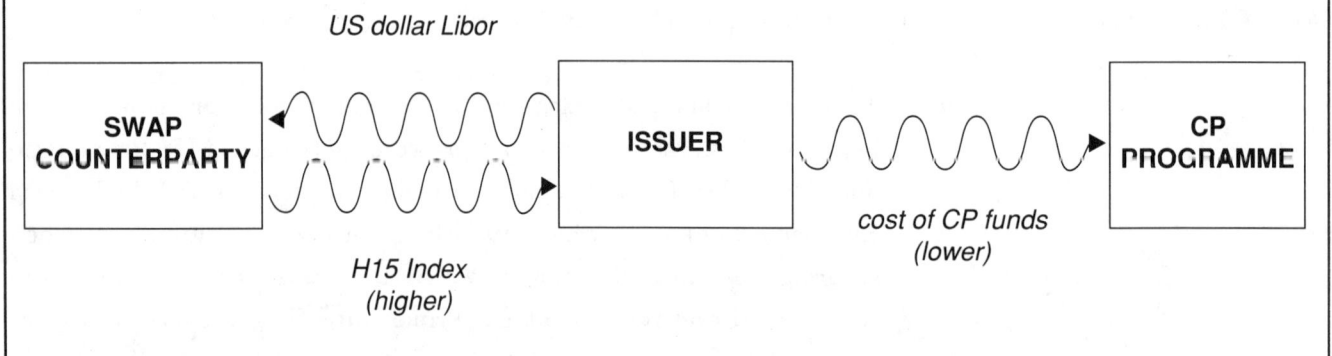

US dollar Libor

| SWAP COUNTERPARTY | | ISSUER | | CP PROGRAMME |

H15 Index
(higher)

cost of CP funds
(lower)

Diagram 20: Hedging basis risk with a basis swap

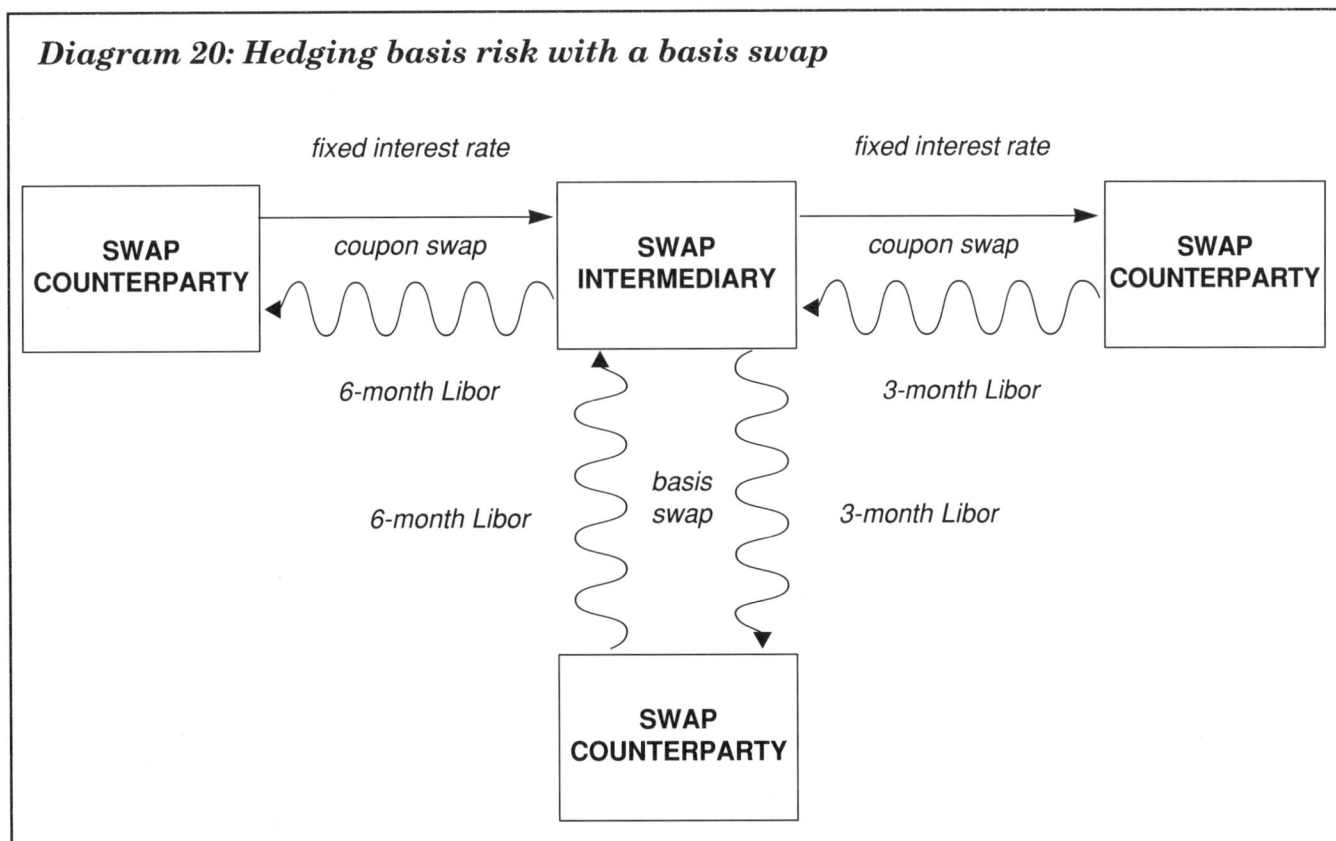

***Constructing
basis swaps***

Intermediaries have tended to create basis swaps in order to hedge the residual basis risk arising from other swaps or within swap portfolios, that is, as by-products of other swap business. Where an intermediary does not have residual basis risk to hedge, a basis swap can be hedged by specially combining generic swaps. Diagram 20 illustrates a basis swap as a hedge against the basis risk created between two coupon swaps with different floating interest rate indexes. In the case of *cross-currency* basis swaps, the combinations of generic swaps used as hedges are called **cocktail swaps** (see the IFR Workbook on *Currency Swaps*).

Pricing basis swaps

Given that basis swaps are usually produced by intermediaries to hedge the residual basis risk arising from other swaps or within swap portfolios, their pricing will tend to reflect how much the intermediary wishes to cover its basis risk exposure and whether the underlying position which is being run is currently in profit or loss, as well as expectations about the future behaviour of the spread between the two floating rate indexes.

Swaps with variable fixed interest

Types and uses of swaps with variable fixed interest

There are two common types of swap which have variable fixed interest rates:

■ **step-up/step-down** swaps;

■ **spreadlock** swaps — sometimes known as 'deferred rate-setting' swaps.

Step-up / step-down bonds

Some bonds — so-called 'graduated-coupon' and 'declining-coupon' bonds — have coupons which increase or decrease in predetermined steps: there is usually just one step up or down. Step-up and step-down swaps are designed to allow the issuers of such bonds to swap into floating interest.

Spreadlock swaps

In markets in which the price of a coupon swap is quoted, like a bond, as a *benchmark yield* plus a *swap spread* (where the benchmark yield is usually that on the most liquid government bond with the same or closest maturity), it is sometimes possible to find swaps in which the swap spread is fixed as soon as the transaction is agreed, but the fixing of the benchmark yield is deferred until later during the life of the swap. The benchmark yield is in fact fixed during an agreed period, but the precise date is otherwise at the discretion of the end-user. The end-user only has the right to choose *when* to fix the benchmark yield during the agreed period, not *if:* a spreadlock swap is therefore a 'time option'. Should the end-user fail to exercise its right to fix the benchmark yield by the end of the agreed period, it is fixed automatically. The option period in spreadlock swaps tends to be between two weeks and six months. Spreadlock swaps are used by borrowers, who swap fixed-interest debt by transacting swaps in which they are receivers of fixed interest:

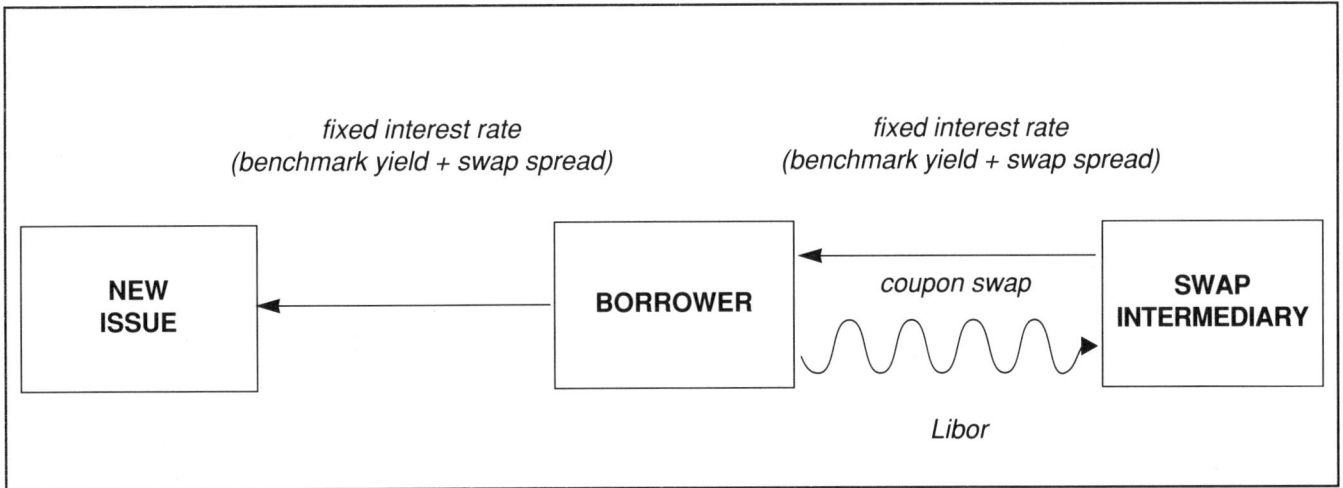

Borrowers will wish to fix swap spreads when these are expected to narrow (as this reduces the interest they receive through swaps), but will wish to defer the fixing of benchmark yields when a general rise in interest rates is expected (as this increases the interest they receive through swaps). Such divergent expectations are normal: changes in swap spreads and interest rates tend to be inversely related. This is because a general rise in interest rates will be reflected in more swap counterparties being willing to receive (higher) fixed interest: this will have the reverse effect of forcing down swap rates, which can only occur by narrowing swap spreads (remember interest rates, including benchmark yields, are rising, so swap rates can only fall by swap spreads narrowing). On the other hand, a general fall in interest rates will be reflected in more counterparties being willing to pay (lower) fixed interest: this will have the reverse effect of bidding up swap rates (remember interest rates, including benchmark yields, are falling, so swap rates can only rise by swap spreads widening). If interest rates are expected to rise and swap spreads to narrow, a counterparty receiving fixed interest through a swap could achieve a higher swap rate by locking in current spreads while they are wide, but deferring the fixing of the benchmark yield till interest rates rise.

Constructing swaps with variable fixed interest

Step-up / step-down swaps

Step-up and step-down swaps can be broken down into combinations of *spot-start swaps* and one or more consecutive *forward swaps*. The component swaps will have fixed interest rates which match the coupons on the underlying bonds. These coupons will be set at off-market rates. The component swaps in step-up or step-down structures will also have to pay off-market fixed interest rates, in order to match cash flows between bonds and swaps. In hedging step-up swaps in which customers are receiving fixed interest, intermediaries face the problem of fixed interest payments to customers through off-market swaps being first lower and then higher (after the step-up) than the fixed interest received from the swaps being used as hedges. Intermediaries will therefore face fixed interest surpluses followed by deficits; and they must temporarily employ the surpluses and then gradually disburse these to fund the deficits.

Spreadlock swaps

Spreadlock swaps are hedged in two parts:

■ The *swap spread* is hedged immediately.

■ The *benchmark yield* is hedged subsequently, as soon as it is fixed by the end-user.

The hedge is in two corresponding parts:

■ The *swap spread* component is hedged with a matching generic swap, which itself is *partially* matched with a temporary hedge (or 'warehouse') of benchmark securities: this partial hedge is against the benchmark yield of the matching generic swap and leaves its swap spread unhedged in order to act as a hedge against the swap spread of the spreadlock swap. In other words:

— the benchmark yield paid by a generic swap is hedged (warehoused) with benchmark securities, leaving its swap spread unhedged;

— the unhedged swap spread paid by the partially-warehoused generic swap is used to hedge the swap spread paid by the spreadlock swap.

■ The *benchmark yield* component of the spreadlock swap is hedged as soon as it is fixed by the end-user, by unwinding the partial warehouse described above and exposing the benchmark yield of the matching generic swap: this leaves in place a permanently matched pair of normal swaps.

The hedging of a spreadlock swap is illustrated in Diagram 21.

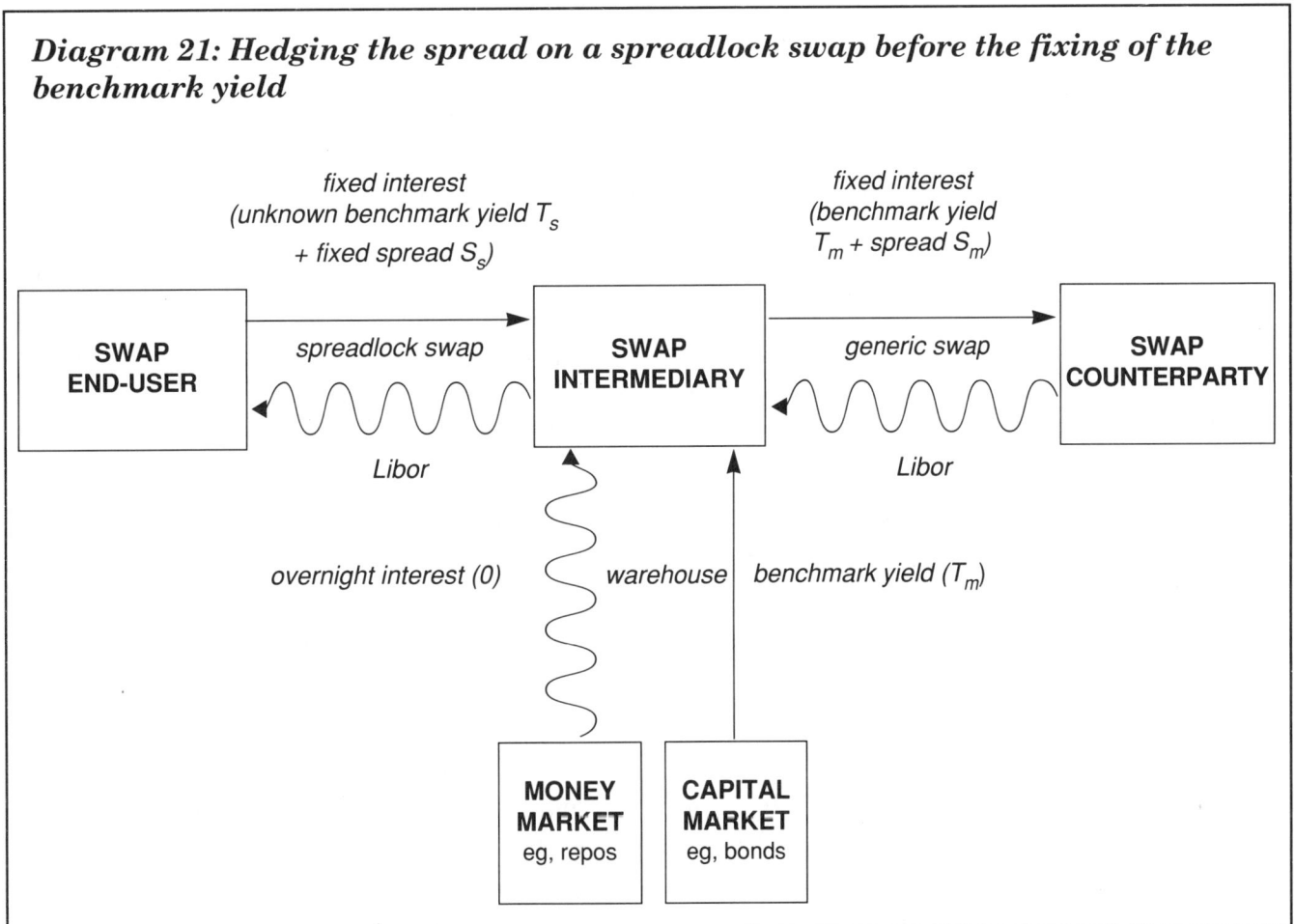

Diagram 21: Hedging the spread on a spreadlock swap before the fixing of the benchmark yield

fixed interest
(unknown benchmark yield T_s
+ fixed spread S_s)

fixed interest
(benchmark yield
T_m + spread S_m)

| SWAP END-USER | spreadlock swap | SWAP INTERMEDIARY | generic swap | SWAP COUNTERPARTY |

Libor

Libor

overnight interest (0)   warehouse   benchmark yield (T_m)

MONEY MARKET eg, repos

CAPITAL MARKET eg, bonds

In this example, the intermediary has transacted a spreadlock swap in which it is the receiver of fixed interest. It has hedged the spreadlock swap with a generic swap in which it is the payer of fixed interest, which is itself partially warehoused with a long position in benchmark securities, which have been financed in the overnight money market (by taking deposits or through repos). If the benchmark yield falls before it is fixed by the end-user, the swap intermediary will receive lower fixed interest through the spreadlock swap than it must pay out through the matching generic swap. This interest loss will, however, be offset by a capital gain on the long position in the benchmark securities.

Pricing spreadlock swaps In the example illustrated in Diagram 21, it can be seen that — until the end-user fixes the benchmark yield of the spreadlock swap — the benchmark component of the fixed interest paid by the intermediary through the matching generic swap (T_m) is funded with the coupons from the warehouse of benchmark securities (T_m), the swap spread of the matching generic swap (S_m) is funded from the swap spread of the spreadlock swap (S_s) and the two Libor cash flows through the two swaps offset each other; which leaves the intermediary to pay overnight interest (O) with the benchmark component of the fixed interest to be received through the spreadlock swap (T_s). Although the benchmark interest to be received through the spreadlock swap will vary until the end-user fixes it, any change will be offset by gains or losses in the capital value of the warehouse of benchmark securities, which means that the fixed interest to be received from the spreadlock swap during the spreadlock period is in fact fixed at the benchmark yield prevailing at the time the spreadlock swap is hedged. If the yield curve is inverted (and overnight rates are higher than the benchmark yield at the start of the transaction), the intermediary will take a loss on this position. This loss is called the *cost of carry* (it is often regarded as the cost of financing the warehouse of benchmark securities at overnight rates). On the other hand, a positive yield curve (in which overnight rates are lower than the benchmark yield fixed at the start of the transaction) will produce a profit on the position, which is described as a *negative* cost of carry. For an intermediary hedging a spreadlock swap with a generic swap in which it pays the fixed and receives floating interest (as in Diagram 21), the cost of carry is:

$$(\text{benchmark yield } (T_m) - \text{overnight rate } (O)) \quad \frac{\text{day count}}{\text{annual basis}} \qquad (1)$$

For an intermediary hedging with a generic swap through it receives fixed and pays floating interest, the cost of carry is:

$$\text{(overnight rate (0) – benchmark yield } (T_m)) \quad \frac{\text{day count}}{\text{annual basis}} \qquad (2)$$

An intermediary should pass on any cost of carry to the end-user by adding a premium to the price of the generic swap and any negative cost of carry by subtracting a discount. However, the cost of carry can only be determined once the hedge is unwound, since the overnight rate will change every day until the end-user fixes the benchmark yield. In estimating how much to charge to cover the cost of carry, intermediaries tend to make the conservative assumption that a spreadlock swap will not be exercised until the end of the spreadlock period. Given the risk that overnight rates may change adversely, intermediaries will often keep any expected cost of carry benefits, in which case, the spreadlock swap may have the same price as a generic swap. However, they may still charge a small risk premium, depending on their expectations about overnight rates.

Swaps with margins over the floating interest rate index

Use of swaps with margins over floating interest rate index

By convention, the floating interest rate in coupon swaps, and also one side of many basis swaps, unless otherwise agreed by the counterparties, is taken to be flat Libor (or the nearest equivalent index, eg Bank Bill Rate in Australia). However, such generic swap structures often give rise to cash flow mismatches against underlying assets or liabilities, exposing end-users to *reinvestment risk:* uncertainty about the total return on an investment due to uncertainty about the rates at which future interest payments can be reinvested for the remainder of the life of the investment. In order to eliminate cash flow mismatches, the swap rate can be brought into line with the interest rate on underlying assets or liabilities. However, adjustments to the swap rate must be compensated by either:

■ a separate *cash payment* (usually made upfront) from the counterparty paying fixed interest at below current market swap rates or receiving fixed interest at above current market rates to the other counterparty;

■ adding or subtracting a *margin* from the floating interest rate index.

The option of making an upfront cash payment is described in the later section on *premium / discount swaps*. This section deals with swaps which pay margins above or below floating interest rate indexes.

An example

Consider the new issue arbitrage, illustrated in Diagram 22a. In this example, a UK building society issues two-year certificates of deposit (CD) at an annual coupon of 12.50% per annum. The swap is against three-month Libor, which is the closest money market proxy to the rate of return on the mortgages which constitute the main assets of the society. The swap rate is 12.65% per annum, so the arbitrage earns an annual turn of 15 basis points (all interest rates are quoted on the same basis). However, the 15 basis points exposes the building society to reinvestment risk. To eliminate this, the swap rate received by the building society is reduced by 15 basis points to 12.50% per annum, to bring it into line with the CD coupon. To compensate the building society, the three-month Libor it pays out through the swap is decreased by the equivalent of 15 basis points. The 15 basis points are paid annually on the fixed interest side of the swap, but three-month Libor is paid quarterly, so it has to be converted from an annual to a quarterly basis: the quarterly equivalent to an annual 15 basis points is in fact 14 basis points[3]. The building society has therefore swapped into floating interest funding at a direct cost of Libor minus 14 basis points.

Pricing swaps with margins over the floating interest rate index

See *Part Two*.

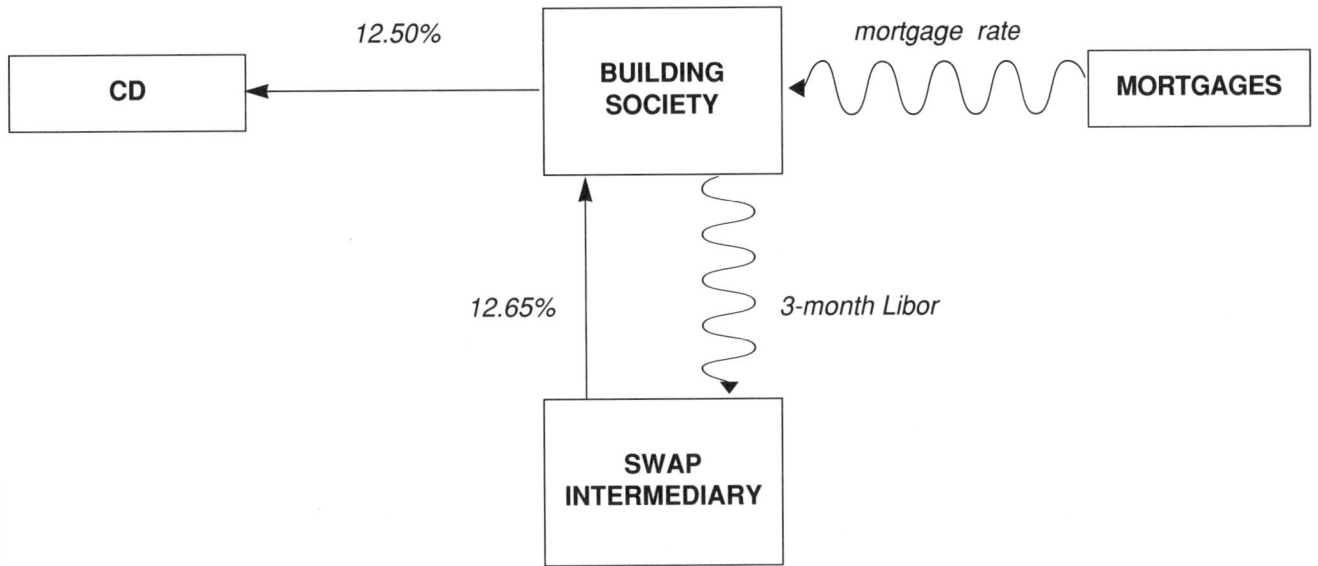

Diagram 22a: Cash flow mismatches in a new issue arbitrage

CD ← 12.50% ← BUILDING SOCIETY ← *mortgage rate* ← MORTGAGES

BUILDING SOCIETY ↑ 12.65% SWAP INTERMEDIARY

BUILDING SOCIETY → *3-month Libor* → SWAP INTERMEDIARY

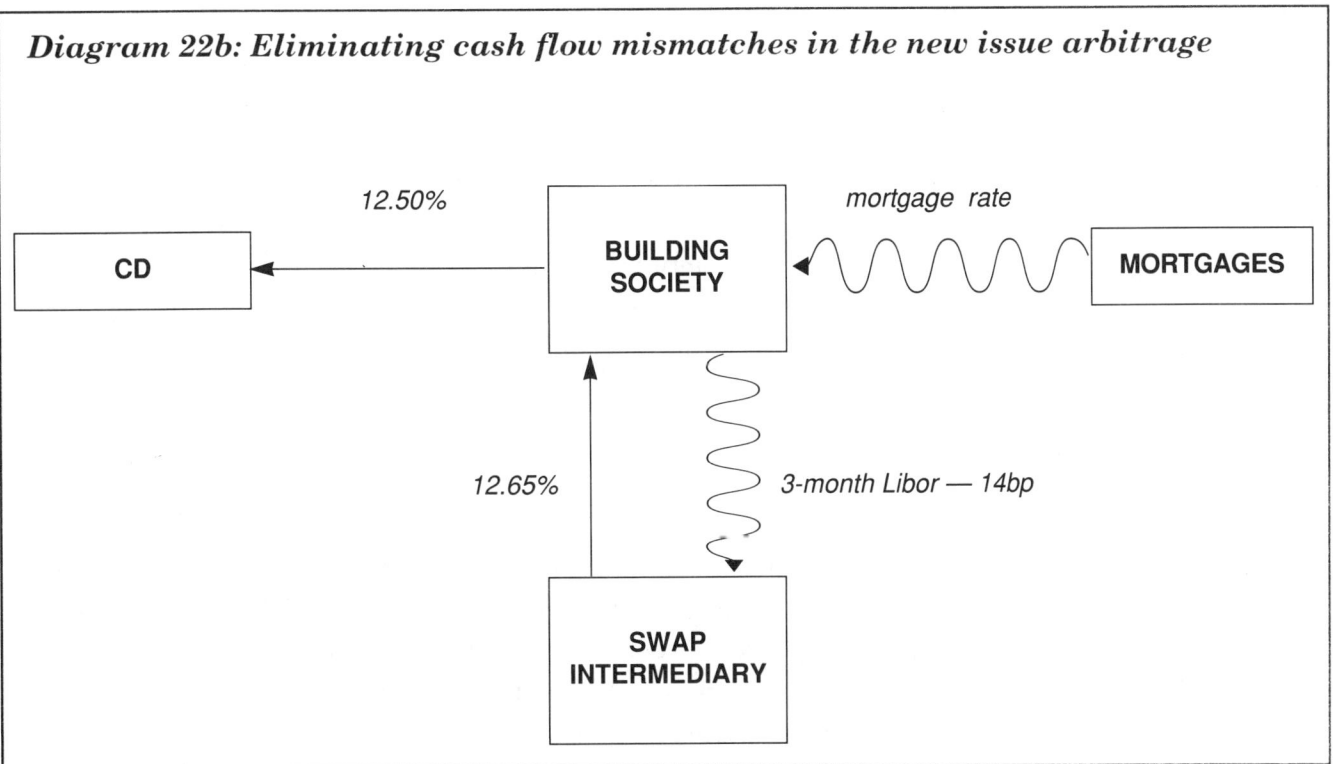

Diagram 22b: Eliminating cash flow mismatches in the new issue arbitrage

CD ← 12.50% ← BUILDING SOCIETY ← *mortgage rate* ← MORTGAGES

BUILDING SOCIETY ↑ 12.65% SWAP INTERMEDIARY

BUILDING SOCIETY → *3-month Libor — 14bp* → SWAP INTERMEDIARY

Swaps with irregular interest payments

Types of swaps with irregular interest payments

There is a range of non-generic swaps with irregular — usually deferred — interest payments:

■   **deferred-coupon bond** swap;

■   **deferred-coupon FRN bond** swap;

■   **zero-coupon** swaps;

■   **premium/discoun**t swaps.

Deferred-coupon bond swaps

Deferred-coupon bond swaps have cash flows designed to match *fixed-income bonds* which pay no coupon for the first few years of the bond. The deferred interest is rolled over and reinvested until the end of the non-payment ('grace') period, when it is paid in a single lump sum. Coupons are then paid normally over the remaining years of the bond.

Deferred-coupon FRN bond swaps

Deferred-coupon FRN bond swaps have cash flows which match special *FRNs* paying no interest in the first years after issue. The deferred interest is rolled over and reinvested until the end of the grace period, when it is paid gradually in the form of a wider margin over Libor in a normal series of interest payments made over the remaining life of the FRN.

Zero-coupon swaps

The zero-coupon swap is the most extreme type of a swap making deferred interest payments: only one payment of interest is made by the counterparty which would normally be the payer of fixed interest. This type of non-generic swap is used in conjunction with underlying zero-coupon securities, where the return to the investor is paid entirely in the form of a capital gain at maturity and includes no interim interest payments.

Premium/discount swaps

Premium and discount swaps involve fixed interest cash flows at *off-market* rates. Premium swaps pay fixed interest at rates above market levels at the time the swap was agreed. Discount swaps pay fixed interest at rates below market levels at the time the swap was agreed. The differential with current swap rates is offset by an upfront payment: if the swap price is below-market, the payer of fixed interest pays an upfront premium as compensation to the receiver and vice versa. Given the usual upfront payment, premium and discount swaps can be regarded as **advanced-coupon swaps**.

The use of swaps with irregular interest payments

Swaps with deferred interest payments are used for a variety of purposes:

■ to defer income for tax purposes in countries where rolled-up interest, along with capital gains, is taxed at more favourable rates than regular interest income;

■ zero-coupon securities avoid the problem of *reinvestment risk* on coupons (ie, uncertainty about the total return on an investment due to uncertainty about the rates at which future coupons can be reinvested for the remainder of the life of the investment);

■ premium or discount swaps are also used for cash flow adjustment.

Constructing swaps with irregular interest payments

There is an essential distinction between swaps with deferred-coupon payments and the advanced-coupon structures represented by premium or discount swaps. The latter involve payments *outside* the structure of the swap to compensate counterparties for the off-market rates paid within the swap, while the former involve the retiming of fixed interest payments within the swap.

Zero-coupon swaps

To construct a non-generic swap with deferred interest payments from a generic swap, the fixed interest cash flows due over the grace period must be rolled-over and reinvested until the end of that period (which is at maturity for zero-coupon transactions), when they are paid as a single lump sum. The cash flow structure of swaps with deferred interest payments is illustrated in Diagram 23, which shows a zero-coupon swap structure.

Diagram 23: Cash flows in a zero-coupon swap

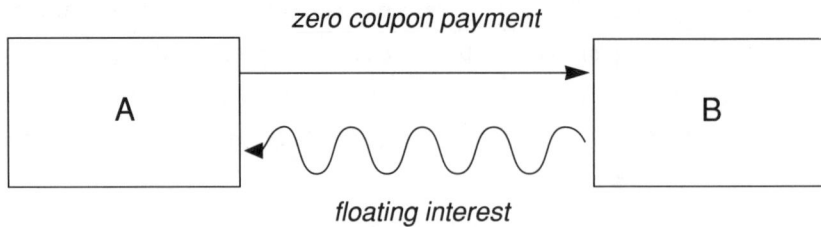

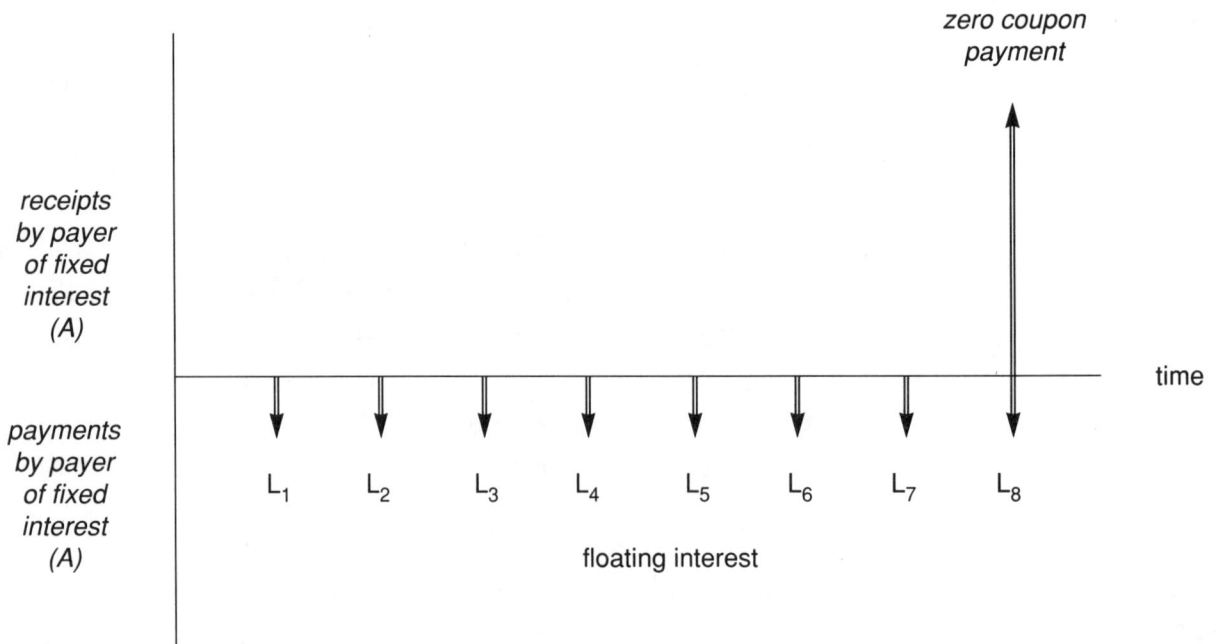

Diagram 23: Cash flows in a zero-coupon swap

Pricing swaps with irregular interest payments

Although deferred-coupon swaps and premium/discount swaps differ in terms of their construction, their pricing differs only in the direction of the calculation:

■ deferred-coupon swaps involve the rolling *forward* and reinvestment of deferred interest;

■ advanced-coupon structures represented by premium/discount swaps involve the calculation of upfront cash payments by discounting *back* to present value the premium or discount between the off-market swap rates paid through these swaps and current market swap rates.

Zero-coupon swaps

The concept of constructing a zero-coupon bond by rolling over, until maturity, the interest cash flows due on a generic swap of the same tenor is simple, but the reality is complicated by reinvestment risk: the interest rate at which each future fixed interest cash flow can be reinvested is unknown in advance and it is therefore impossible to calculate the amount of the payment at maturity with certainty, unless the future reinvestment rates are fixed, eg, with forward swaps.

An example

The pricing of a zero-coupon swap is illustrated in Table 7. This calculates the price of a zero-coupon swap which is equivalent, in terms of the value of fixed

Table 7: Pricing a zero-coupon swap

Year	Fixed interest payments through swap per $1 notional principal amount at swap rate of 7% pa	Cash interest rates (%pa)	Forward-forward interest rates (%pa)	Cumulative balances from the reinvestment at forward-forward interest rates of fixed payments paid at end of year:				
				1	2	3	4	5
1	7.000	5.0		7.000				
2	7.000	5.5	6.00	7.420	7.000			
3	7.000	6.0	7.01	7.940	7.491	7.000		
4	7.000	6.5	8.01	8.576	8.091	7.561	7.000	
5	7.000	7.0	9.02	9.350	8.820	8.243	7.631	7.000
	35.000			zero-coupon payment (sum of balances at end of year 5)				41.044
				rate of return over 5 years (US$41.044/US$100.00)				41.044%
				zero-coupon swap rate (% pa)				7.12

interest payments made by each, to a normal swap priced at 7% per annum. It is assumed that each fixed interest payment through the normal swap is reinvested at the prevailing forward-forward interest rates (implied here from prevailing cash interest rates)[4]. The sum of these reinvestments gives the equivalent zero-coupon payment, from which an annual zero-coupon swap rate is calculated.

Premium/discount swaps

The upfront cash payments which compensate counterparties for off-market swap rates they pay or receive through a premium/discount swap are simply the NPV of those premiums or discounts. Because a stream of fixed interest payments is a series of constant amounts, its NPV can be calculated as an annuity, using the formula:

$$PMT \; \frac{1 - (1 + \frac{R}{f.100})^{-n}}{\frac{R}{f.100}} \qquad (3)$$

where   PMT = amount of fixed interest payment
        R = discount rate
        f = frequency of payments per year
        n = number of payments during the swap

The discount rate used in calculating NPV is the current market swap rate. The NPV of the premiums or discounts between the off-market swap rates paid through premium/discount swaps and current market swap rates is simply the difference between the NPV of the off-market interest stream and the current market interest stream. This is paid to the counterparty receiving below-market fixed interest through the swap.

An example

Consider a three-year premium swap with a notional principal amount of US$10m which pays fixed interest annually at 9% per annum (an annual payment of US$900,000) against Libor. Assume current market swap rates are 8% per annum[4]. The NPV of the fixed interest stream paid through the premium swap is:

$$\$900,000 \; \frac{1 - (1 + \frac{8}{100})^{-3}}{\frac{8}{100}} \; = \$2,319,387 \qquad (4)$$

The NPV of the fixed interest stream paid an equivalent swap priced at current market rates is:

$$\$800{,}000 \ \frac{1-(1+\frac{8}{100})^{-3}}{\frac{8}{100}} = \$2{,}061{,}678 \tag{5}$$

The difference between the two NPVs is US\$257,709. This amount is usually paid upfront in cash. As the receiver of fixed interest through the premium swap is getting more than current market swap rates, it makes the upfront payment to the payer of fixed interest.

Swaps with deferred start dates

Types and uses of swaps with deferred start dates

There are two basic types of interest rate swap which involve start dates later than the usual 'spot' start (meaning two business days after a transaction has been agreed):

■ **delayed-start** swaps — also known as 'deferred-takedown' or 'forward commencement' swaps;

■ **forward** swaps.

Delayed-start swaps

In a delayed-start swap, the terms and conditions of the transaction are agreed now, but will not come into effect (ie, interest will not start accruing) until a *future* date, although this will be *within six months* of the deal being agreed. Such swaps are used to fix future swap rates in order to anticipate future underlying transactions, if interest rates are expected to move adversely before these transactions can be undertaken. Thus, a delayed-start swap would be transacted, if interest rates were expected to fall in advance of a bond issue which is to be swapped into a floating liability (a fall in rates would otherwise mean the issuer receiving fixed interest through the swap at less than current rates). Delayed-start swaps can also be used to match the interest periods of existing underlying transactions more closely.

Forward swaps

A forward swap is similar in concept to a delayed-start swap in that it does not come into effect until a *future* date, but this will be *more than six months* after the deal is agreed, perhaps as much as three years. Forward swaps are classified into:

■ straight forward swaps — delayed start swaps through which fixed interest is *paid*;

■ *reverse* forward swaps — delayed start swaps through which fixed interest is *received*.

Forward swaps can be used, like delayed start swaps, to fix future swap rates in order to anticipate future underlying transactions, if interest rates are expected to move adversely before these transactions can be undertaken. Thus, a forward swap (in which fixed interest is paid) would be transacted, if interest rates are expected to rise in advance of making a fixed-interest investment which is to be swapped into a floating rate asset (otherwise, fixed interest paid through the swap would be higher than necessary) or raising floating-interest funding to be swapped into fixed-rate liabilities (otherwise, fixed interest received through the swap would be lower than necessary).

Constructing delayed-start swaps

The principle of constructing a delayed-start swap is illustrated in Diagram 24. A delayed-start swap is hedged with a matching generic spot-start swap with the same maturity: the intermediary accepts the exposure to interest rate risk over the period of the delay until the delayed-start swap comes into effect (although it might hedge this). This means it will have to cover any losses on the matching swap during this period.

Diagram 24: Constructing a delayed-start swap

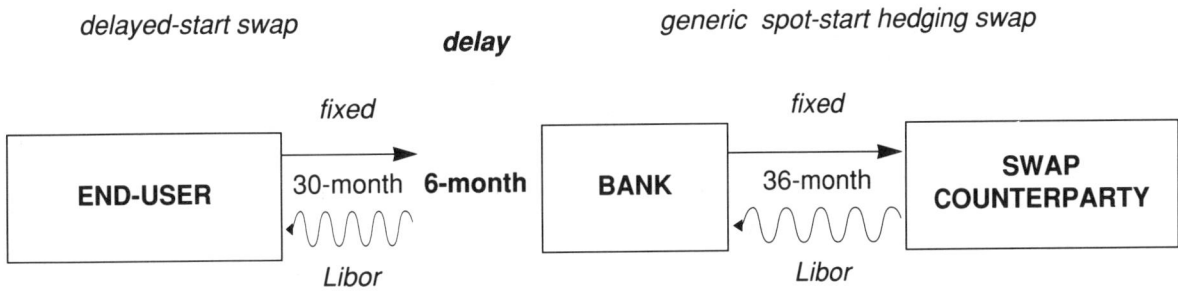

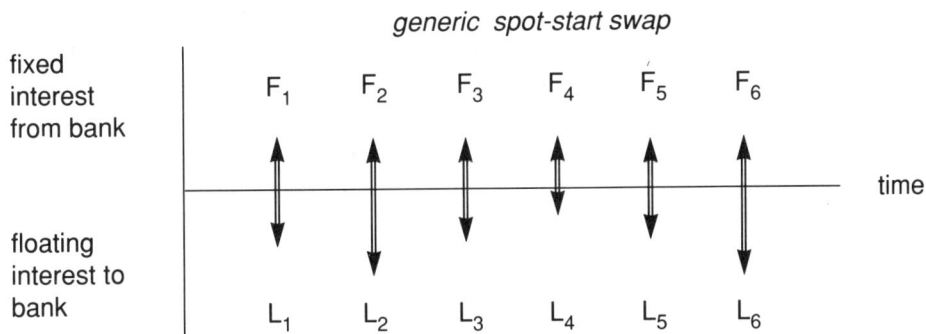

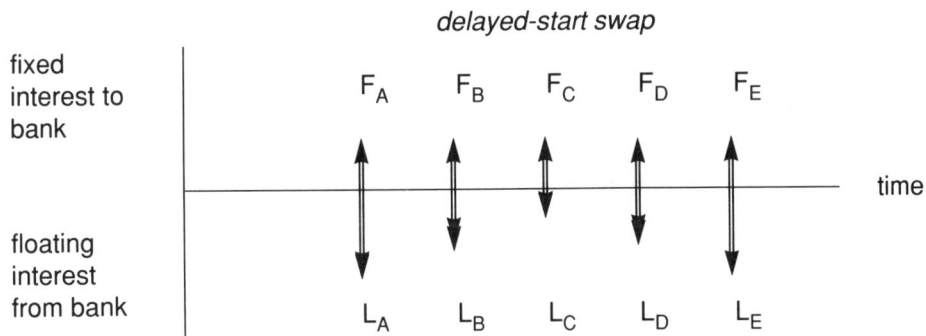

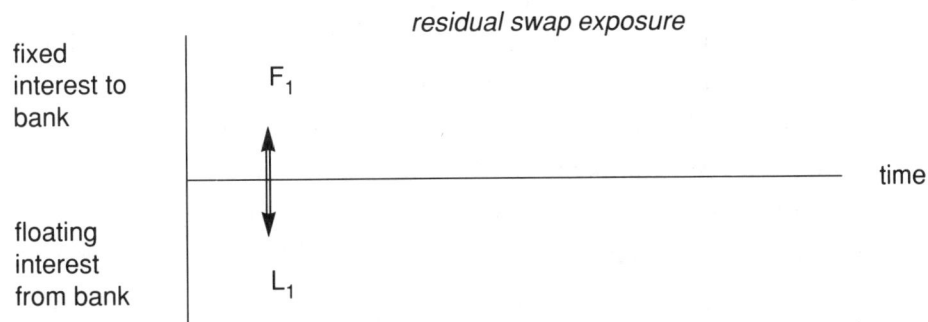

delayed-start swap   **delay**   generic spot-start hedging swap

fixed   fixed

| END-USER | 30-month **6-month** | BANK | 36-month | SWAP COUNTERPARTY |

Libor   Libor

generic spot-start swap

fixed interest from bank

F_1 F_2 F_3 F_4 F_5 F_6

time

floating interest to bank

L_1 L_2 L_3 L_4 L_5 L_6

delayed-start swap

fixed interest to bank

F_A F_B F_C F_D F_E

time

floating interest from bank

L_A L_B L_C L_D L_E

residual swap exposure

fixed interest to bank

F_1

time

floating interest from bank

L_1

Pricing delayed-start swaps

As noted, a delayed-start swap is hedged with a generic spot-start swap with the same maturity, with the intermediary accepting the interest rate exposure during the delay until the delayed-start swap comes into effect. The price of a delayed-start swap must therefore take into account any losses or profits on the matching swap during the period of the delay. A loss — called the *cost of carry* — is the difference between the interest paid and received through the swap, and is the cost of financing the swap. A profit is described as a negative cost of carry. An intermediary will pass on any cost of carry to the end-user in the form of a premium on the price of the generic swap and any negative cost of carry in the form of a discount. For an intermediary hedging a delayed-start swap with a generic swap in which it pays fixed and receives floating interest (as in Diagram 24), the cost of carry is:

$$\text{cost of carry} = (\text{fixed rate} - \text{floating rate}) \, \frac{\text{day count}}{\text{annual basis}} \qquad (6)$$

For an intermediary hedging with a generic swap through it receives fixed and pays floating interest, the cost of carry is:

$$\text{cost of carry} = (\text{floating rate} - \text{fixed rate}) \, \frac{\text{day count}}{\text{annual basis}} \qquad (7)$$

Thus, if the fixed interest rate is lower than the floating rate — which would be the case if the yield curve were inverted — an intermediary hedging a delayed-start swap with a generic swap in which it pays fixed and receives floating interest (as in Diagram 24) will benefit from a negative cost of carry. The price of the delayed-start swap will therefore be the price of the generic swap less a discount equal to the cost of carry over the period of delay. If, on the other hand, the yield curve is positive, the same intermediary will face a negative cost of carry and the price of the delayed-start swap will be the price of the generic swap plus a premium equal to the cost of carry over the period of delay.

An example

Take the example illustrated in Diagram 24. Assume that the price of the generic swap is 9.60% and Libor is six-month Libor, which is currently fixed at 9.80%pa[4] — in other words, an inverted yield curve. Also assuming 30-day months and a 360-day year, the cost of carry to the swap intermediary is:

$$\text{cost of carry} = (9.60\% - 9.80\%)\,\frac{180}{360} = -0.10\%\text{pa} \tag{8}$$

The cost of carry (which in this case is a negative) is then amortised over the term of the delayed-start swap to calculate the discount to be deducted from the three-year generic swap rate in order to give the price of the 30-month delayed-start swap.

Constructing forward swaps

A forward interest rate swap, like other forward-forward instruments, is a maturity mismatch between two opposing generic spot-start instruments of different tenors. The two swaps largely cancel out for the spot period over which they coincide, leaving the swap intermediary with a net exposure over the forward-forward period for which the longer-term swap exceeds the shorter-term swap. The intermediary uses this forward-forward exposure to hedge the forward swap offered to the customer. The concept is illustrated in Diagram 25 below. Here the intermediary transacts opposing generic two-year and four-year swaps. These largely cancel out for the spot two-year period, but leave residual risk (the remnant of the spot four-year swap) over the forward-forward period between two and four years. This is used to hedge a forward swap for a customer over the same forward-forward period.

Diagram 25: Constructing a forward swap

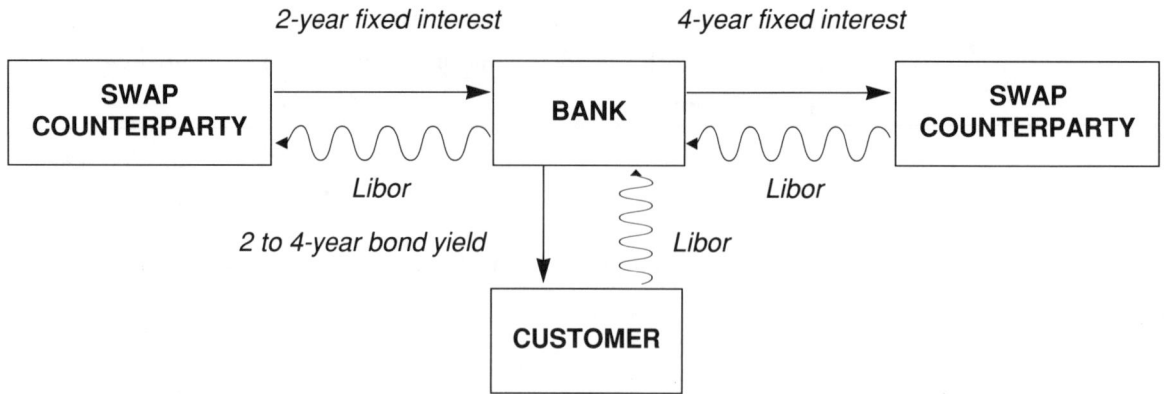

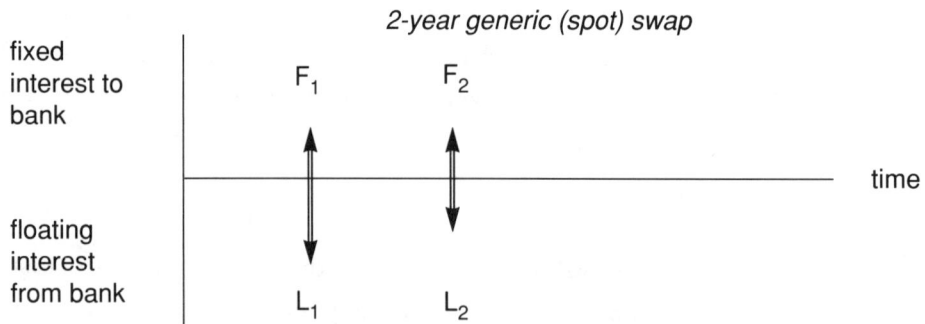

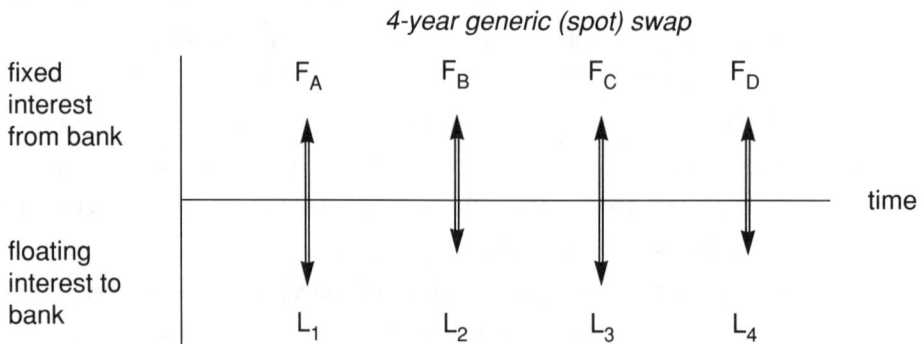

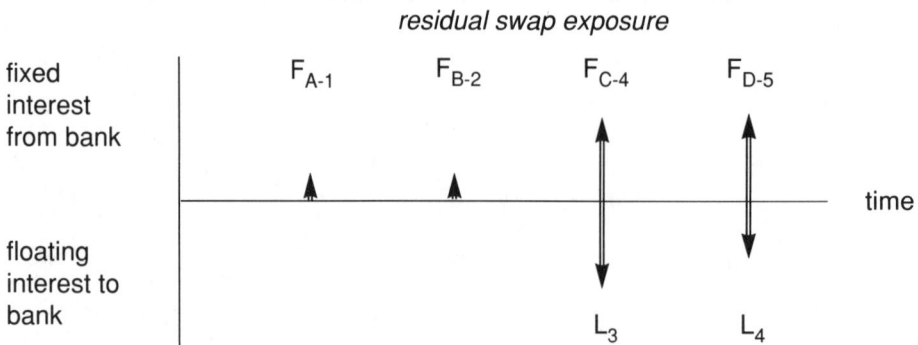

2-year fixed interest   4-year fixed interest

| SWAP COUNTERPARTY | → | BANK | → | SWAP COUNTERPARTY |

Libor   *Libor*

2 to 4-year bond yield   *Libor*

CUSTOMER

2-year generic (spot) swap

fixed interest to bank F_1 F_2 time

floating interest from bank L_1 L_2

4-year generic (spot) swap

fixed interest from bank F_A F_B F_C F_D time

floating interest to bank L_1 L_2 L_3 L_4

residual swap exposure

fixed interest from bank F_{A-1} F_{B-2} F_{C-4} F_{D-5} time

floating interest to bank L_3 L_4

Pricing forward swaps

Given that a forward swap can be constructed by transacting two opposing generic spot-start swaps of differing maturities, its price is composed of:

■ any differential between the generic swap prices for the *spot* period over which they are coincident, which may be due to:

— dealing spread;

— differences in tenor, the effect of which depends on the slope of the yield curve.

■ price of the longer-term generic swap over the *forward-forward* period with which it is not coincident and not offset by the shorter-term generic swap.

The price of that part of the longer-term generic swap not offset by the shorter-term generic swap forms the basis of forward swap price. To this is added or subtracted any differential between the generic swap prices for the spot period over which the two generic swaps coincide and offset.

An example

Take the forward swap illustrated in Diagram 25 above, which is a two-year swap starting in two years and thus maturing in four years. Assume the two-year generic swap price is 8.00%pa and the four-year spot generic price is 9.00%pa[4]. Further assume that the floating interest rate index for both generic swaps and the forward swap is 12-month Libor. The cash flows involved in constructing the forward swap in the above example, as seen from the point of view of the intermediary, are set out in Table 8 below. The basic forward swap price is the price of the four-year generic swap in years 3 and 4. On top of this, a premium is added to reflect the fact that the two generic swaps leave the intermediary paying a net differential of 1.00%pa over the two years for which they coincide. The premium is calculated by amortising, over the term of the forward swap (years 3 and 4), the NPV of the net differential (over years 1 and 2).

Table 8: Pricing a forward swap

| Period years | 2-year spot swap | | 4-year spot swap | | forward swap | |
	receive fixed	pay floating	pay fixed	receive floating	pay fixed	receive floating
1	+8.00%	−Libor	−9.00%	+Libor	+1.00%	0
2	+8.00%	−Libor	−9.00%	+Libor	+1.00%	0
3	—	—	−9.00%	+Libor	+9.00%	−Libor
4	—	—	−9.00%	+Libor	+9.00%	−Libor

Swap derivatives

Swap futures

In June 1991, the Chicago Board of Trade (CBOT) introduced futures and options contracts on three and five-year US dollar interest rate swaps. In effect, these instruments are *highly-standardised, exchange-traded* delayed-start swaps. The idea is to provide an organised market as an alternative to the OTC market in which swaps have hitherto been traded.

The mechanics of the contracts

The CBOT futures contracts are not measured in terms of the notional principal amount of the notional underlying swap. Instead, the trading unit is measured in terms of *yield:* the contracts gain or lose US$25 for every half basis point change in yield. The way this method works can be seen from an example.

An example

Consider the three-year US dollar interest rate swap illustrated in Diagram 26.

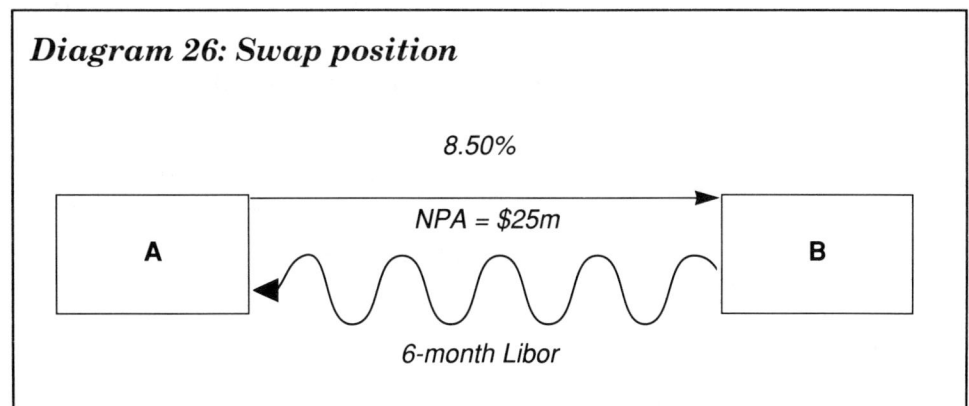

Diagram 26: Swap position

8.50%

A

NPA = $25m

B

6-month Libor

The notional principal amount of the swap is US$25m and the swap rate is 8.50% per annum (paid semi-annually) against six-month Libor. Assume current swap rates are 8.45% per annum. If interest rates were to rise by one basis point, the value of the swap to counterparty B would fall and to A would rise by US$6,505: see Table 9.

Table 9: Calculating the change in swap value per basis point

Year	$ value of 1 basis point on $25 million	$ value of interest payment discounted at 8.45%
0.5	1,250	1,199
1.0	1,250	1,151
1.5	1,250	1,104
2.0	1,250	1,059
2.5	1,250	1,016
3.0	1,250	975
net present value of 1bp		6,505

The counterparties could hedge with interest rate swap futures. Given that swap futures gain or lose US$25 per one-half basis point, in order to compensate for a loss of US$6,505 per one basis point, the intermediary would need US$6,505/US$50 = 130 contracts. Counterparty B would in fact have to *sell* swap futures in the example. This is because the price of the contracts is quoted as an index of 100 minus the swap rate (eg, a swap price of 8.45% per annum should be reflected in a futures price of 100 – 8.45 = 91.55): a hedge against a rise in interest rates — which would reduce futures prices — involving selling contracts in order to buy them back again at lower levels to make hedging profits.

Contract specifications

The price of the swap futures contract is quoted as an index of 100 minus the swap price. The swap price at which the CBOT contracts is settled is defined as an average of those quoted to prime US banks for generic par swaps with a notional principal amount of US$25m. The notional swaps which underlie the CBOT futures contracts mature on the third Wednesday of one of the four traditional quarterly contract months (in March, June, September and December). Swap prices are the all-in prices (average of the bid and offer) taken from seven banks randomly selected from a list. The floating interest rate index is six-month US dollar Libor. Fixed and floating interest payments are assumed to be made simultaneously every six months. Settlement involves the payment of the net difference between the price at which a futures contract was transacted and the settlement price. The specifications of the contracts are summarised in Table 10.

The CBOT swap futures have not performed well. The three-year contract did not trade at all in 1992 and the five-year contract traded only 2,389 contracts, with little open interest. The contracts have not traded at all in the first quarter of 1993.

Table 10: Specifications for CBOT swap futures contracts

Contract parameter	3-year swap future	5-year swap future
Underlying swap	forward 3-year par coupon swap	forward 5-year par coupon swap
Notional principal amount of underlying swap	varies with swap price	varies with swap price
Fixed interest rate on underlying swap	forward price for 3-year swaps with NPA of $25 million to prime US banks (bid/offer average)	forward price for 5-year swaps with NPA of $ 25 million to prime US banks (bid/offer average)
Floating index on underlying swap	6-month Libor	6-month Libor
Assumed payment frequency of underlying swap (fixed and floating)	semi-annually and simultaneously	semi-annually and simultaneously
Quotation of futures price	100 – swap price	100 – swap price
Contract tick size (value of a basis point price change)	$25/0.5 basis point	$25/0.5 basis point
Contract months	March, June, September, December	March, June, September, December
Last trading day	Monday before third Wednesday of contract month	Monday before third Wednesday of contract month
Settlement day	third Wednesday of contract month	third Wednesday of contract month
Delivery day	last trading day of contract month	last trading day of contract month
Delivery method	cash settlement at exchange settlement price	cash settlement at exchange settlement price

Options on swaps

Definition	An option on a swap is a contract which gives the buyer the right, but does not impose any obligation on it, to enter into a forward swap with the seller, or extend or terminate an existing swap with the seller, in exchange for the payment of a premium by the buyer to the seller.

The choice which is given to the buyer of an option on a swap — whether or not to enter, extend or maintain a swap — means that:

- if the underlying swap is expected to generate a *loss*, the buyer of the option can back out of the swap: an option to enter a forward swap can be allowed to expire unexercised, or an option to terminate an existing swap can be exercised;

- but, if the underlying swap is expected to generate a *profit*, the buyer can go through with the swap: an option to enter a forward swap or extend an existing swap can be exercised, or an option to terminate an existing swap can be allowed to expire unexercised.

In contrast, counterparties to non-optional instruments (like FRAs, futures and non-optional swaps) are obliged to go through with these transactions, whether they are expected to generate profits *or* losses. In other words, options have asymmetric risk-return (limited loss, if prices move adversely; unlimited profit, if prices move favourable), whereas non-optional instruments are symmetric (unlimited loss, if prices move adversely; unlimited profit, if prices move favourably).

Risk-return asymmetry is a characteristic, not only of options, but also of *insurance*, and analogies are often drawn between the two instruments. An option hedge allows the buyer to keep profits, but compensates for losses. Similarly, an insurance policy does not require the insured party to share the increased value of the insured object with the insurance company, but it does compensate for losses. Also like insurance, options tend to be expensive (and both charge a 'premium').

Terminology

Options on swaps use standard option terminology:

- The end of the option period is called the **expiry date**.

- The fixed interest rate on the underlying swap is called the **strike rate**.

- The level of interest rates at which the underlying swap starts to move from loss into profit, or vice versa, is called the **break-even rate**. This is different from the strike rate because of the cost of the premium. For example, consider an option on a three-year swap with a notional principal amount of US$100m and a strike rate of 8% per annum. Assume the premium is 2%: this is a flat percentage of the principal amount, so the swap needs to earn

  US$100m x 2% = US$2m

  just to cover the premium. A premium of US$2m for a three-year swap is equivalent to 66 basis points per annum (US$2m amortised at 8% per annum over three years). Assuming the buyer of the option would pay fixed and receive floating interest through the swap — so that interest rates would have to rise to make the swap profitable — the break-even rate would be:

  8% + 66 basis points = 8.66% per annum

Types of options on swaps

Options are available on a number of types of swap: interest rates, currencies, equities and physical commodities. An option on an interest rate swap is a type of *interest rate option*. Other interest rate options are combinations of different instruments. Thus, *interest rate guarantees* combine options and FRAs, and *listed (exchange-traded) options* combine options and futures. The CBOT *interest rate swap futures options* are combinations of three types of instrument. Options on swaps are *OTC* instruments and were developed after listed interest rate options had been established. As OTC instruments, options on swaps avoid some of the problems posed by listed interest rate options: inflexible terms (in respect of notional principal amounts, maturities, strike rates and choice of interest rates); cumbersome administrative procedures like margining; the restriction of trading to exchange; and the fact that the underlying instruments in listed options are government securities, which do not cover spreads over government yields and therefore expose users to *spread risk*.

Options on swaps differ in terms of the rights of the holder of the option with regard to the underlying swap:

- A **swaption** is an option to *enter* into a forward swap and *pay fixed interest*. The term swaption has sometimes been used for customer transactions and the term 'callable swap' for interbank swaptions. A swaption tied to specific securities may be called a **contingent swap**.

- An **extendible swap** is an option to *enter* into a forward swap and *receive fixed interest*. It is therefore the opposite of a swaption and may be called a *put swaption* (as it *puts* the right to pay fixed interest with the counterparty).

- A **callable swap** is an option to *extend* an existing swap.

- A **putable swap** is an option to *terminate* an existing swap. It is therefore the opposite of a callable swap.

This terminology is not universal and great care needs to be taken in the use of names for options on swaps. Conventions differ within and between financial centres.

Table 11: Types of options on swaps

Type of option	Alternative names	Right of holder	
Swaption	call swaption contingent swap [callable swap]	to enter swap	to pay fixed
Extendible swap	put swaption		to receive fixed
Callable swap		to extend swap	
Putable swap	terminable swap cancellable swap	to terminate swap	

Like other options, options on swaps can differ in terms of *when* they can be exercised:

■ **American**-style options can be exercised at any time up to the expiry date;

■ **European**-style options can be exercised only on the expiry date.

The basic structure of the different types of options on swaps is compared in Diagram 27.

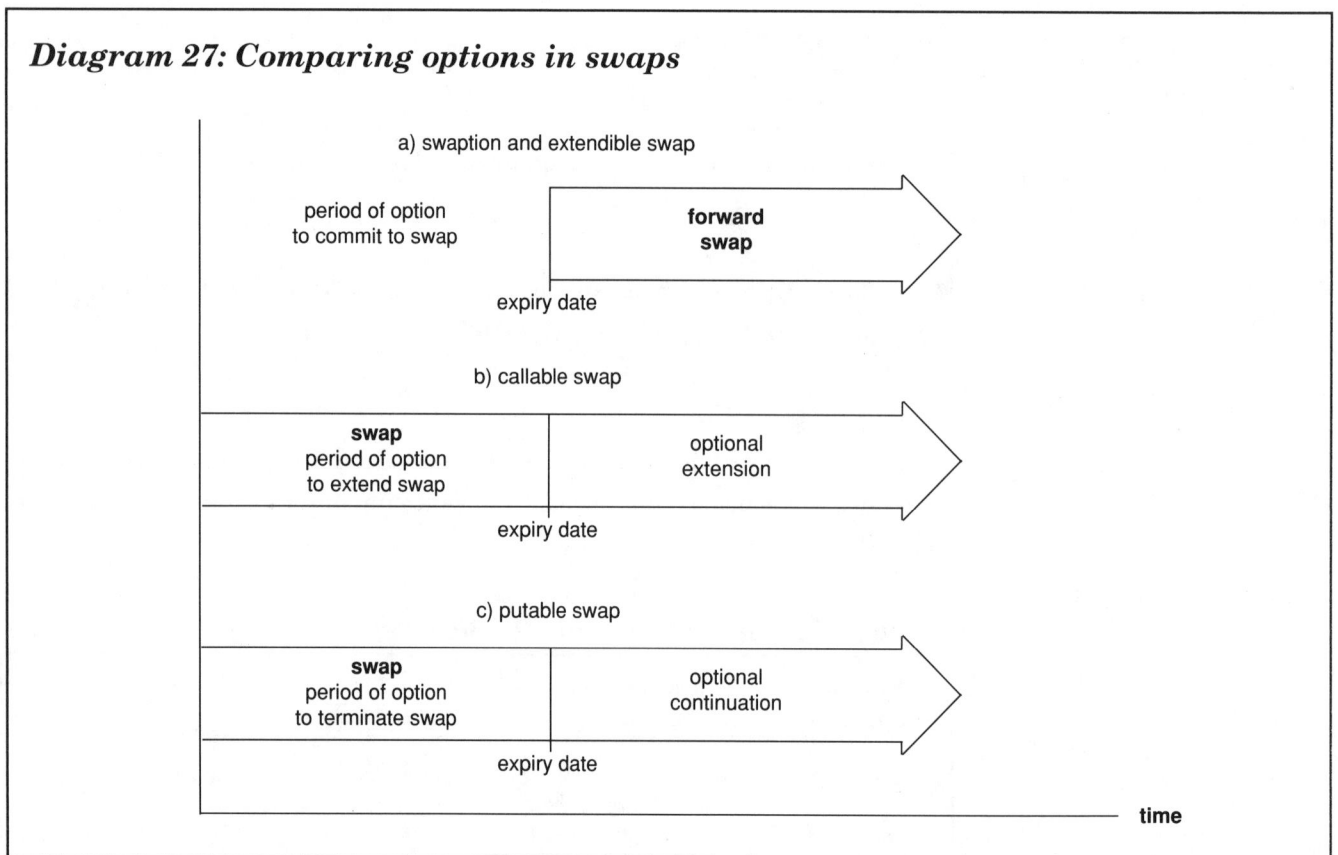

Diagram 27: Comparing options in swaps

a) swaption and extendible swap

period of option
to commit to swap

forward swap

expiry date

b) callable swap

swap
period of option
to extend swap

optional
extension

expiry date

c) putable swap

swap
period of option
to terminate swap

optional
continuation

expiry date

time

Uses of options on swaps   The asymmetric risk-return on an option — limited loss, if prices move adversely; unlimited profit, if prices move favourably — makes the instrument ideal for managing high risk situations.

Management of risk in volatile markets

Options are particularly useful in situations of intense price **volatility**. When the *direction* of future interest or exchange rate movements is uncertain, but the *range* of these movements (in either or both directions) is expected to be wide, the risk of adverse price movements and unlimited losses is high, but so is the opportunity of favourable price movements and unlimited profits. Only an option can provide the possibility of profits, while limiting the risk of loss.

While the option in an option on a swap provides insurance against adverse price movements, the underlying swap is used, like any swap, for the conventional purposes of taking risk positions on favourable price movements or hedging against the risk of adverse price movements.

An example

Consider a company with a US$25m bank loan which is priced at six-month Libor plus 100 basis points and which has exactly five years to run. Assume the company believes that short-term interest rates will ease for the next year and will then trend upwards for the remaining four years of the loan, eventually exceeding 10% per annum. In order to fix its borrowing cost in the last four years of the loan, the company would normally put on a four-year forward swap starting in one year, in which it pays fixed interest and receives Libor. However, the company also believes that short-term interest rates will be very volatile, so it chooses a swaption rather than a conventional swap. This is illustrated in Diagram 28.

Diagram 28: Using a swaption

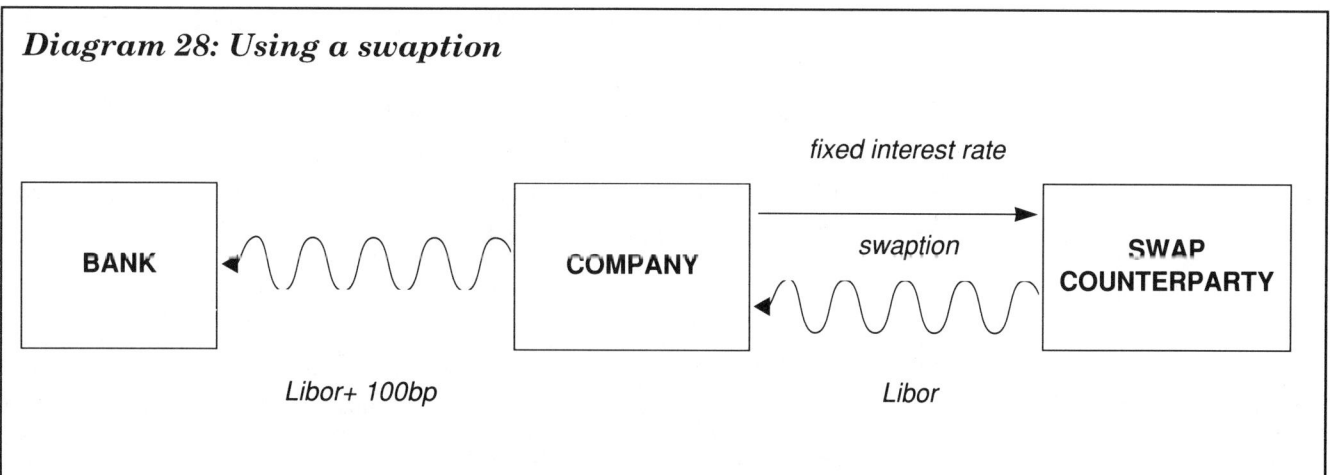

Current six-month Libor is 6% per annum and the company's borrowing cost is therefore 7% per annum. Ideally, the company would hedge 6% per annum. However, the closer the swap rate is to current market rates, the more likely it is to be reached and the option exercised, so the greater the premium which will be required by the seller of the option for taking the risk. The swap rate will reflect a balance between the protection which is desired by the option buyer and the premium which can be afforded. The company decides to absorb any increase in its borrowing costs up to 12% per annum, which implies Libor of 11% per annum. However, as noted already, the company has to take into account the fact that the premium will erode the profitability of the underlying swap. Therefore, in order to achieve protection against Libor of 11% or more — in other words, to achieve a *break-even rate* of 11% — the company has to buy a swaption with a strike rate lower than 11% per annum by the amount of the premium amortised over the life of the swap. An illustrative outcome would be the company buying a swaption with a strike rate of 10.56% per annum for which it pays a premium of 1 3/4% (which is equivalent to 0.35% per annum when amortised over four years at the current Libor of 6% per annum). Once Libor reaches the strike rate of 10.56% per annum, profits will start to accrue on the swap. These profits make it worthwhile to exercise the option, as they recoup some of the premium. When Libor reaches the break-even rate of 11% per annum, the option premium will have been fully covered and net profits will start to accrue to the company, providing compensation for further interest rate rises.

Assume the company revised its view about future interest rates before its swaption expired and now believed that short-term interest rates over the next five years would trend downwards. The company would no longer need the swaption. However, rather than let it expire unexercised, the company could sell the swaption and recoup some of the original premium. While there is any time left till expiry, an option will have value. This is true even when the underlying instrument would be unprofitable to transact, as there will be time for unexpected price movements to push it into profit.

Management of risk associated with uncertain events

Options are also appropriate instruments for hedging where it is uncertain that the event to be hedged will occur. The classic example of this type of situation is the 'tender-to-contract' period of a construction project. In tendering for a project, the bidder needs to fix the cost of financing by hedging with a swap or similar instrument at the time of the tender. However, if the bidder does not win the contract, a swap transacted during the tender would not be a hedge, but a risk in its own right. An option on a swap or similar instrument provides a solution: the option could be left to expire unexercised if the bid failed.

In the capital market, an example of an uncertain event is provided by securities with options embedded in them which allow early redemption by the issuer (*callable bonds*) or the investor (*putable bonds*). This means issuers or investors wishing to swap from fixed to floating interest do not know what maturity of swap to put on. For example, if a five-year bond has a three-year call option, there is a dilemma about whether to use a three or five-year interest rate swap. A three-year swap will be too short, if the call option is not exercised; a five-year swap too long, if it is. The solution is to put on a conventional three-year swap and a three-year option to enter a two-year swap (a swaption or callable swap). Or, the issuer could buy a five-year swap with a three-year option to terminate (a putable swap).

Another example of an uncertain event in the capital market is provided by *bond warrants*. These are securitised options to buy bonds at an agreed price during an agreed period. The issuer of warrants might wish to swap any bonds issued through the exercise of its warrants from a fixed to a floating interest basis, but it cannot be sure whether, or even when, the warrants will be exercised by investors. The solution is for the issuer to buy a callable swap, with an option having the same expiry as the warrants and an underlying swap having the same maturity as the bonds underlying the warrants. If the callable swap is tied to specific warrants, it is called a *contingent swap*.

Other uses of options on swaps: arbitrage

One of the driving forces behind the development of options on swaps has been the **new issue arbitrage** opportunities provided by differences between the price of options in the bond market (in the form of embedded options) and in the market in options on swaps. This sort of arbitrage is illustrated in Diagram 29. The arbitrage involves:

■ the issuer issuing a *callable bond* and paying investors a premium for the embedded call option which is implicit in the higher yield: the call option gives the issuer an opportunity to redeem the bond before maturity and refinance at lower interest rates;

■ the issuer sells a *putable swap*, usually to an options market intermediary, in return for a premium: the putable swap gives its buyer the right to terminate the swap; the underlying swap also commences immediately, like a conventional instrument, swapping the fixed interest payment obligations of the issuer on its bond into floating interest (the swap into floating interest allows the issuer to benefit from falling interest rates, while the call option in its bond provides it with insurance against rising interest rates).

The putable swap is the reverse of the embedded call option and the two should therefore hedge each other. Thus, a fall in interest rates below the swap rate will push the swap into loss, which should encourage its buyer to exercise its put option and terminate the swap. However, the fall in interest rates should also prompt the issuer to exercise the call option on its bonds in order to be able to refinance at lower interest rates. This will mean that the issuer no longer needs the swap, but (as explained already) this should be terminated by the issuer's counterparty. As the two options will be exercised simultaneously, they can be seen to cancel each other out. The arbitrage opportunity in this situation depends on whether there is any difference between the implicit premium paid by the issuer on the embedded call option in its bond and the explicit premium received by the issuer on the putable swap it has sold. Price differences do in fact occur between embedded call options and putable swaps, because investors have tended to undervalue the call options embedded in callable bonds when compared with the value put on the equivalent option in putable swaps by option market intermediaries.

Diagram 29: Arbitrage between an embedded call option and a putable swap

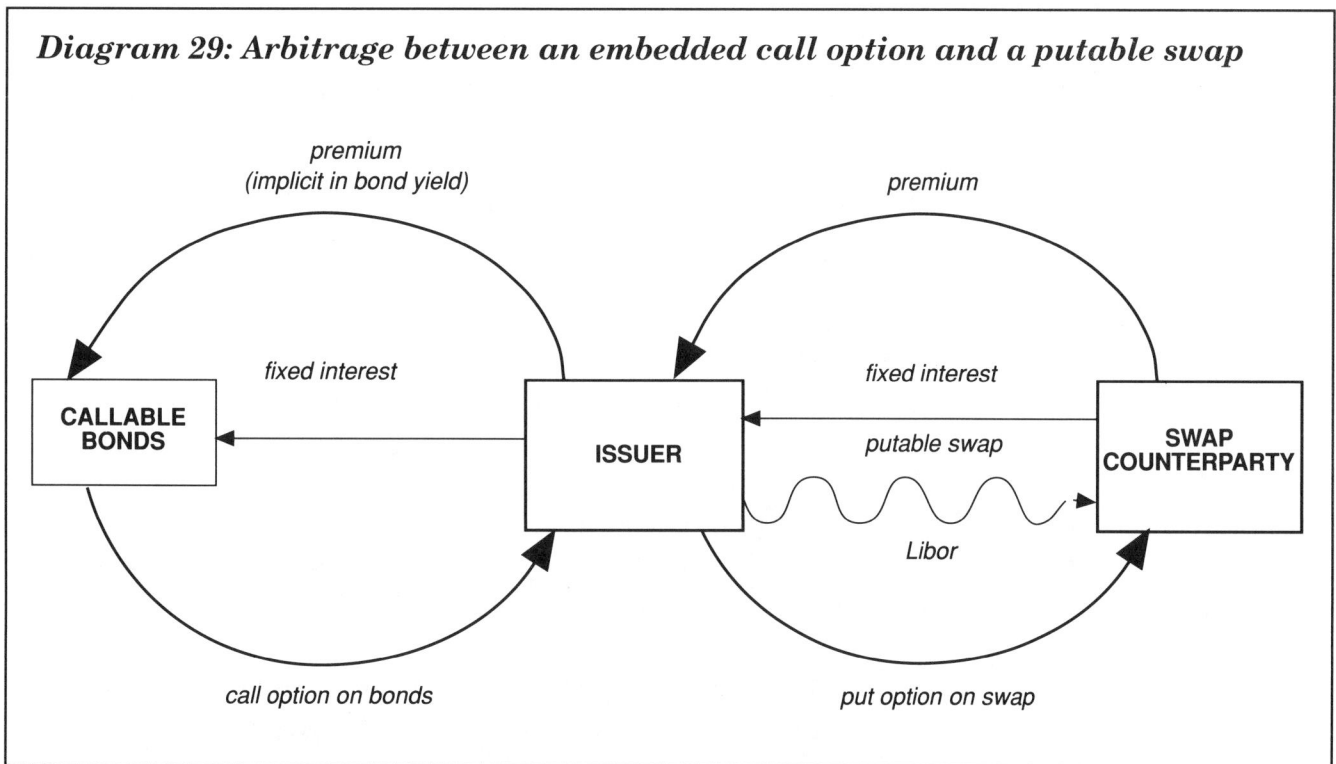

premium
(implicit in bond yield)

premium

fixed interest

fixed interest

| CALLABLE BONDS | | ISSUER | | SWAP COUNTERPARTY |

putable swap

Libor

call option on bonds

put option on swap

Constructing options on swaps

As explained already, the swaps which underlie options on swaps are in themselves conventional swaps, which are used like conventional swaps and have the same features in terms of:

■   notional or actual *principal amounts*;

■   *periods*;

■   *swap rates*;

■   *swap structure* (eg, interest rate or currency swap, coupon or basis swap, floating interest rate index, etc).

The options which are attached to the swaps are conventional options: their pricing, transaction mechanism and terminology are generally the same as for options on other commodities.

Pricing options on swaps

The pricing of options on swaps is based on conventional option pricing methods (which are not covered in this Workbook) and reflects the same factors:

■ strike rate

■ current market swap rate

■ maturity of the swap

■ option period

■ American or European-style option

■ volatility of swap prices

The prices of options on swaps tend to reflect the prices of bond options, given that these provide the principal means of hedging options on swaps. For example, an intermediary selling a swaption, and therefore accepting the risk of having to receive the fixed and pay floating interest through the swap, will hedge against the risk of higher interest rates by buying a put option on bonds. If interest rates do rise, the put option on bonds will increase in value (since it entitles bonds to be sold at a fixed and higher price), which will compensate for the higher floating interest paid through the swap. However, the securities underlying bond options are government bonds. Hedging options on swaps with bond options therefore suffers from the same *swap spread risk* as hedging conventional swaps with government bonds.

Notes

1. The Federal Reserve Commercial Paper Composite Index — the so-called 'H-15' Index — is an average of quotes from six large dealers of US CP issued by companies with bond ratings of Standard and Poor's AA or the equivalent, obtained at 11:00am each day and published by the Federal Reserve Board in its weekly H-15 bulletin.

2. The Kenny Index is a weekly index of average 30-day yield evaluations at par of not less than 20 issues of high-grade securities issued by municipal, local and other government bodies which are exempt from Federal income tax and are selected by Kenny Information Systems.

3. The formula for converting from an annual to a quarterly basis for compounding interest is:

$$\left(\sqrt[4]{\left(1 + \frac{PA}{100}\right)} - 1 \right) 400$$

4. All interest rates are quoted on the same basis in terms of day count, annual basis and compounding conventions.

Self-Study Exercises: <u>Questions</u>   Part 3

Question 3.1:   What are the seven key characteristics that define a non-generic swap?

Question 3.2:   By what other names are generic and non-generic swaps more popularly known in the market?

Question 3.3:   Briefly define each of the following types of non-generic swap:

- amortising swap

- accreting swap

- roller-coaster swap

- basis swap

- step-up/step-down swap

- spreadlock swap

- deferred-coupon swap

- deferred-coupon FRN swap

- premium/discount swap

- zero-coupon swap

- delayed-start swap

- forward swap

Question 3.4: Calculate the price of a three-year amortising swap, paying fixed interest annually against 12-month Libor, with a notional principal amount of US$60m which decreases each year by one-third. Current generic swap rates are:

1 year	9.20%
2 years	9.35%
3 years	9.57%

Question 3.5: If three-year basis swaps between US Prime Rate and Libor are quoted as '–85/–81', what are the absolute interest rates paid through the swap?

Question 3.6: Outline the construction of a *spreadlock swap*.

Question 3.7: What is the price of a three-year *zero-coupon swap* with a notional principal amount of US$8m, given the following current bond yields:

1-year bond yield	7.25%
2-year bond yield	7.65%
3-year bond yield	7.83%

Question 3.8: Outline the construction of a *delayed-start swap*.

Question 3.9: What is the price of a one-year against three-year *forward swap*, given the following current generic swap rates:

1-year swap rate	8.36%
2-year swap rate	8.66%
3-year swap rate	8.89%

Question 3.10: Outline a new issue arbitrage against a callable bond.

Self-Study Exercises: <u>Answers</u>   Part 3

Answer 3.1:   The seven key characteristics of a non-generic swap are:

■ constant principal amount (*notional* principal amounts in interest rate swaps and *actual* principal amounts in currency swaps);

■ an exchange of fixed for floating interest or — in the case of some currency swaps — fixed for fixed interest;

■ any fixed rate of interest is constant;

■ any floating rate of interest is flat;

■ payments of interest are made regularly;

■ interest starts accruing no later than spot value;

■ no special risk features.

(Total marks = 7 marks)

Answer 3.2:   ■ Generic swaps are popularly known as *straight* or *plain vanilla* swaps.

(1 mark)

■ Non-generic swaps are popularly known as *exotic* swaps.

(1 mark)

(Total marks = 2)

Answer 3.3:   ■ *amortising swap*: principal amount decreases in steps;

■ *accreting swap*: principal amount increases in steps;

- *roller-coaster swap*: principal amount increases and then increases in steps;

- *basis swap*: exchange of two floating interest streams;

- *step-up/step-down swaps*: the fixed interest rate in the swap increases or decreases in steps;

- *spreadlock swap*: the swap spread is fixed immediately, but the benchmark yield can be fixed at the discretion of one of the counterparties any time during an agreed period after the start of the swap;

- *deferred-coupon swap*: fixed interest payments (coupons) are deferred for an initial period after the start of the swap; at a later date, when regular coupon payments start, the deferred interest (plus reinvestment interest) is paid as a lump sum;

- *deferred-coupon FRN swap*: floating interest payments are deferred for an initial period after the start of the swap; at a later date, when regular interest payments start, the deferred interest is paid in the form of an extra margin over normal interest payments;

- *zero-coupon swap*: only one payment is made on what would normally be the fixed interest side of the swap and this occurs at maturity;

- *delayed-start swap*: while the terms of the swap are agreed immediately, the swap does not start until an agreed date in the future, usually within six months of the transaction being agreed;

- *forward swap*: similar to a delayed-start swap, but starting more than six months after the transaction is agreed.

(Total marks = 11)

Answer 3.4: The calculation of the price of the amortising swap is set out in the table. The amortising swap is constructed by combining generic swaps with maturities of one, two and three years, each with a notional principal amount of US$20m. The price is a weighted average of the prices of the three generic swaps, where the weights are tenor and notional principal amount.

Tenor (years)	Principal amount of amortising swap (million)	Principal amount of component generic swap (million)	Swap price (% pa)	Principal amount of generic swap weighted by tenor (million)	Principal amount of generic swap weighted by tenor and swap price (million)
spot	60				
1	40	20	9.20	20	1.840
2	20	20	9.35	40	3.740
3	0	20	9.57	60	5.742
sub-totals				120 (A)	11.322 (B)
weighted average swap rate (= (B)/(A) x 100)					**9.435%pa**

(Total marks = 6)

Answer 3.5: The intermediary quoting a Prime/Libor basis swap at '–85/–81' is willing to transact US dollar swaps in which it either:

■ pays the current US Prime Rate less 85 basis points — in return for receiving Libor flat;

(1 mark)

■ receives the current US Prime Rate less 81 basis points — in return for paying Libor flat.

(1 mark)

(Total marks = 2)

Answer 3.6: A *spreadlock swap* is constructed from a two-part hedge (which is illustrated in the diagram below):

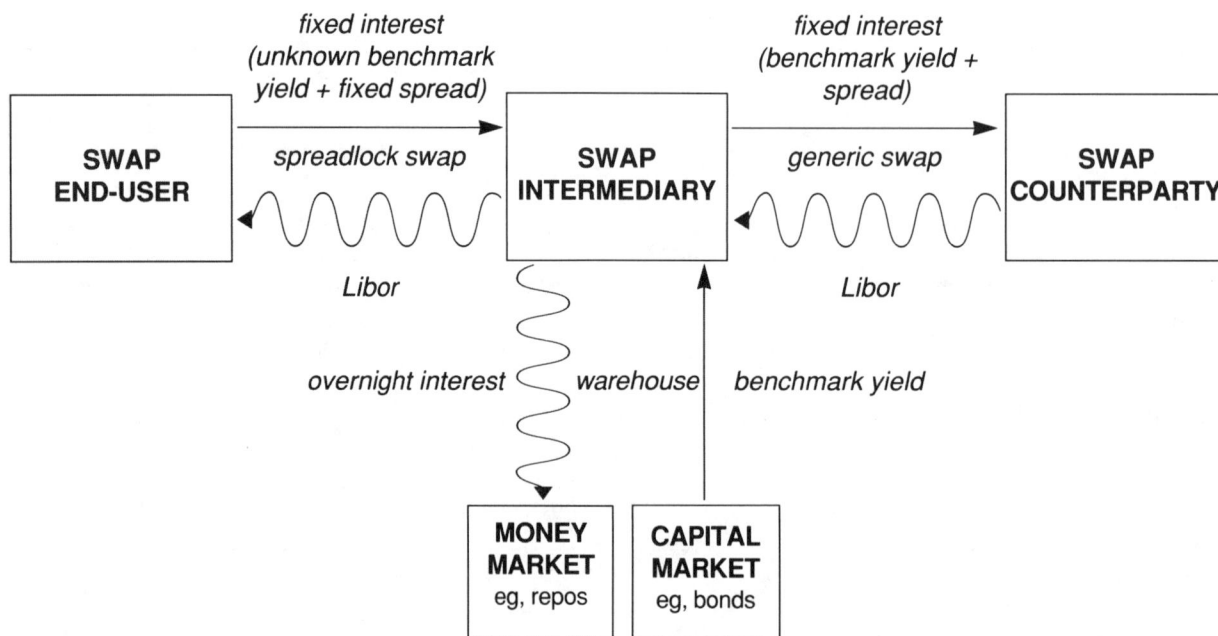

(3 marks)

- The *swap spread* — which is fixed immediately — is hedged with a matching generic swap, which itself is *partially* matched with a temporary warehouse of benchmark securities: this partial hedge is against the benchmark yield of the matching generic swap and leaves its swap spread unhedged in order to act as a hedge against the swap spread of the spreadlock swap. In other words:

  — the benchmark yield paid through a generic swap is warehoused with benchmark securities, leaving its swap spread unhedged;

  (2 marks)

  — this unhedged swap spread is then used to hedge the swap spread paid through the spreadlock swap.

  (2 marks)

■ The *benchmark yield* of the spreadlock swap — which is fixed after the start of the swap, at the discretion of one of the counterparties — is only hedged when it is fixed. This is done by unwinding the partial warehouse described above and exposing the benchmark yield of the matching generic swap to leave in place a permanently matched pair of normal swaps.

(2 marks)

(Total marks = 9)

Answer 3.7: The calculation of the price of the zero-coupon swap is set out in the table. The zero-coupon swap is constructed by rolling over, until maturity, the interest cash flows which would be due on a generic swap of the same tenor. The interest rate at which each future fixed interest cash flow can be reinvested is unknown in advance (giving rise to reinvestment risk), unless future reinvestment rates are fixed. In the example, reinvestment is fixed at forward-forward interest rates implied from cash interest rates.

Year	Fixed interest payments through swap per $1 notional principal amount at swap rate of 7.83% pa	Cash interest rate (% pa)	Forward-forward interest rates (% pa)	Cumulative balances from the reinvestments at forward-forward interest rates of fixed interest payments paid at end of year:		
				1	2	3
1	0.626400	7.25%	—	0.626400		
2	0.626400	7.65%	8.05%	0.676825	0.626400	—
3	0.626400	7.83%	8.19%	0.732257 (A)	0.677702 (B)	0.626400 (C)
	1.879200			zero-coupon payment (sum of balances at end of year 3 = A+B+C)		2.036359
				rate of return over 3 years (US$2.036359/US$8.0)		25.454%
				zero-coupon swap rate		7.85%pa

(Total marks = 9 marks)

Answer 3.8: The principle of constructing a delayed-start swap is illustrated in the diagram. A delayed-start swap is hedged with a matching generic spot-start swap with the same maturity. However, the spot-start swap covers the period before a delayed-start swap comes into effect and so poses a risk to the intermediary. The intermediary has to accept the exposure to interest rate risk over this period before the delayed-start swap comes into effect and has to cover any losses on the spot-start swap during this period (although he may try to hedge this).

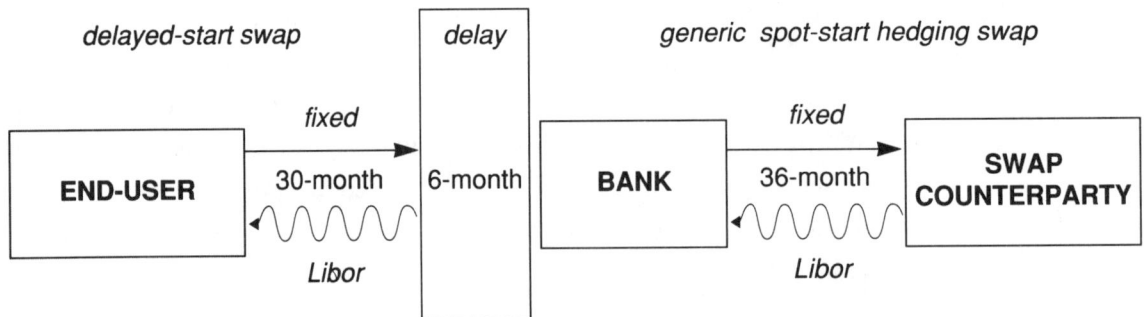

(Total marks = 4)

Answer 3.9: The cash flows involved in constructing the forward swap are set out in the table.

Period (years)	1–year spot swap		3-year spot swap		Forward swap	
	receive fixed	pay floating	pay fixed	receive floating	pay fixed	receive floating
1.0	+8.36%	–Libor	–8.89%	+Libor	+0.53%	0
2.0	—	—	–8.89%	+Libor	+8.89%	–Libor
3.0	—	—	–8.89%	+Libor	+8.89%	–Libor

The premium is then calculated by amortising, over the term of the forward swap (years 2 and 3), the net present value of the net differential (over year 1).

(Total marks = 6)

Answer 3.10: A new issue arbitrage against a callable bond involves two opposite transactions:

■ An issuer issues a *callable bond* and pays investors a premium for the embedded call option which is implicit in the higher yield. The call option allows the issuer to redeem the bond before maturity and refinance at lower interest rates;

(2 marks)

■ The issuer sells a *putable swap* in return for a premium. The putable swap gives its buyer the right to terminate the swap, which commences immediately and swaps the fixed interest paid by the issuer on its bond into floating interest.

(2 marks)

The putable swap is the reverse of the embedded call option and the two should therefore hedge each other. Thus, a fall in interest rates below the swap rate will push the swap into loss for the swap counterparty (which pays fixed interest and receives floating), which should encourage the counterparty to exercise its put option and terminate the swap. However, the fall in interest rates should also prompt the issuer to exercise the call option on its bonds in order to be able to refinance at lower interest rates. This will mean that the issuer no longer needs the swap, but (as explained already) the counterparty will also be seeking to terminate the swap. As the two options will be exercised simultaneously, they can be seen to cancel each other out. The arbitrage opportunity in this situation depends on whether there is any difference between the implicit premium paid by the issuer on the embedded call option in its bond and the explicit premium received by the issuer on the putable swap it has sold.

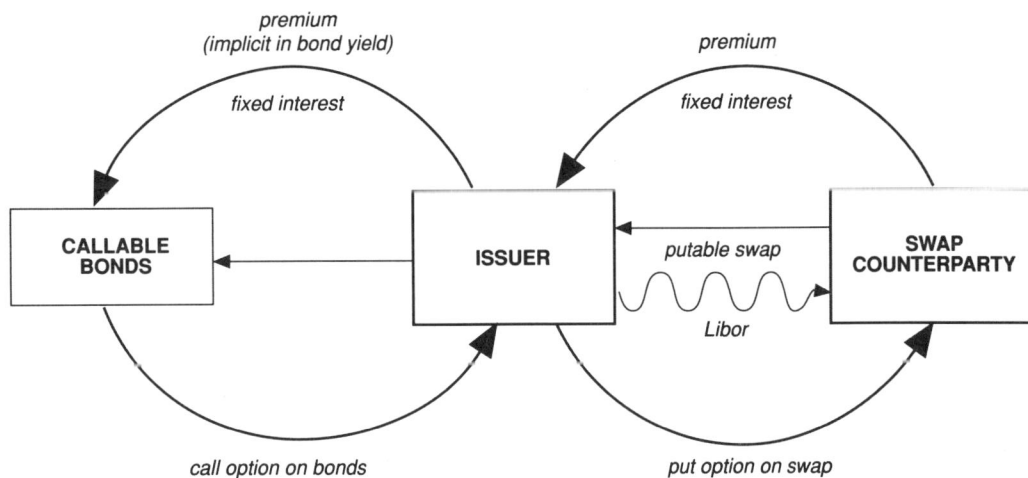

premium
(implicit in bond yield)

premium

fixed interest

fixed interest

CALLABLE BONDS

ISSUER

putable swap

SWAP COUNTERPARTY

Libor

call option on bonds

put option on swap

(Total marks = 4)

Glossary

Accreting swap

Interest rate or currency swaps with notional or actual principal amounts (notional in the case of interest rate swaps and actual in the case of most currency swaps) which increase in steps over the life of the swap. *cf amortising swap*

Amortising swap

Interest rate or currency swaps with notional or actual principal amounts (notional in the case of interest rate swaps and actual in the case of most currency swaps) which decrease in steps over the life of the swap. *cf accreting swap*

Asset swap

An asset swap is an interest rate or currency swap which is attached to an asset.

Basis swap

An interest rate or currency swap involving an exchange of two streams of payments, each calculated using different floating interest rate indexes. Basis swaps can be between:

■ *different tenors* of the same index, eg, three-month Libor against six-month Libor;

■ same or different tenors of *different indexes*, eg, three-month US dollar Libor against three-month US Treasury bill yield or six-month US dollar Libor against US Prime Rate;

■ an index and its *average*, eg, six-month Libor against the weekly average of six-month Libor over six months.

Basis swaps between different currencies are often called *cross-currency basis swaps*. Basis swaps are sometimes called *index* swaps.

Callable swap

An interest rate or currency swap with an option to extend its life. Sometimes used instead to describe interbank *swaptions*. *cf putable swap*

Cancellable swap

Another name for a *putable swap*.

Contingent swap

Another name for a *swaption* tied to specific securities.

Deferred-coupon bond swap

An interest rate or currency swap with cash flows which match those on a bond which pays no coupon for the first few years of its life, but then pays coupons normally over the remaining years.

Deferred-coupon FRN bond swap

An interest rate or currency swap with cash flows which match special floating-rate notes (FRNs) paying no interest in the first years after issue, but then paying a wider margin over Libor in a normal series of interest payments made over its remaining life.

Delayed-start swap	An interest rate or currency swap in which the terms and conditions of the transaction are agreed now, but do not come into effect (ie, interest will not start accruing) until a future date, although this will be within six months of the deal being agreed. See also *forward* swap.
Discount swap	An interest rate or currency swap which involves fixed interest cash flows at off-market rates. Discount swaps pay fixed interest at rates below market levels at the time the swap was agreed. The differential with current swap rates is offset by an upfront payment from the payer of fixed interest to the receiver. *cf premium swap*
Extendible swap	An interest rate or currency swap with an option to enter into a forward swap in which the option holder has the right to receive fixed interest. Sometimes called a *put swaption. cf swaption*
Financial engineering	A multi-disciplinary approach to the management of risk and return which involves the use of derivative instruments — particularly swaps — to decompose standard financial transactions into their elements and then synthesise these elements into innovative cross-market structures customised to the particular requirements of counterparties.
Forward swap	An interest rate or currency swap similar in concept to a *delayed-start* swap, in that it does not come into effect until a future date, but this will be more than six months after the deal is agreed, perhaps as much as three years. Forward swaps are classified into:

■ straight forward swaps — delayed start swaps through which fixed interest is paid;

■ *reverse* forward swaps — delayed start swaps through which fixed interest is received.

Generic swap

An interest rate or currency swap which has the simplest structure possible. Specifically, a generic swap has all of the following characteristics:

■ constant principal amount (notional principal amounts in interest rate swaps and actual principal amounts in currency swaps);

■ an exchange of fixed for floating interest or — in the case of some currency swaps — fixed for fixed interest;

■ any fixed rate of interest is constant;

■ any floating rate of interest is 'flat' — in other words, there is no margin over the floating rate index;

■ payments of interest (fixed or floating) are made regularly;

■ interest starts accruing no later than for 'spot' value (ie, two business days after the transaction is agreed);

■ no special risk features (eg, attached options).

Investor asset swap

An asset swap with the simplest possible transaction structure. The investor organises and is placed at the centre of the structure. An intermediary may propose the asset swap to the investor, sell it the asset and act as its swap counterparty, but the intermediary takes no other responsibility. This structure poses a number of practical problems for the investor:

■ The investor is responsible for the **administration** of the complex set of cash flows.

■ The investor is exposed to the **credit risk** of both the issuer of the asset and the swap counterparty.

■ **Accounting** is likely to be complex, probably requiring separate treatment of the cash asset and the swap, which may distort the perceived benefit of the transaction.

■ The **liquidity** of the asset swap depends on the liquidity of the swap and the asset, and the structure has to be liquidated in two parts, involving two sets of transactions costs.

These drawbacks tend to mean that investor asset swap structures are the preserve of the more sophisticated institutional investor.

Packaged asset swap

Another name for a *synthetic security*.

Premium swap

An interest rate or currency swap with fixed interest cash flows at off-market rates. Premium swaps pay fixed interest at rates above market levels at the time the swap was agreed. The differential with current swap rates is offset by an upfront payment to the payer of fixed interest through the swap from the receiver. *cf discount swaps*

Putable swap

A swap with an option to terminate it. *cf callable swap*

Reinvestment risk

Uncertainty about the total return on a swapped asset arising because of differences between the coupon received on the asset and the fixed interest paid through the swap. Because future interest rates are unknown, it is uncertain at what rates net interest gains will be reinvested. Reinvestment risk in asset swaps is solved with *premium* or *discount* swaps, or swaps paying a margin against the floating interest.

Repackaged security

Asset swaps in which investors receive, not just a cash flow on the swapped asset, but the swapped asset itself in the form of a negotiable security. For this reason, repackaged securities are also known as *securitised asset swaps*. Repackaged securities are generally created through one-off companies, usually incorporated in an offshore tax haven, called *special purpose vehicles (SPV)*, established to buy and hold an asset and put on a swap with the intermediary organising the repackaging, and then issue new securities which reflect the characteristics of the swapped asset. The proceeds of the new issue are used to fund the purchase of the assets being swapped and these are used to collateralise the new issue. Apart from adding liquidity to asset swaps in the form of the repackaged security, repackaging reduces the credit risk taken by the intermediary, which is no longer exposed to the investor through the swap.

Reset swap

A *basis swap* between a floating interest rate index and its average, eg, six-month Libor against its weekly average over six months. The frequent refixing of the index makes it behave like a very short-term interest rate and it is a partial substitute for an overnight rate.

Roller-coaster swap

A swap which is a combination of an amortising and accreting swap: the principal amount increases in steps and then decreases in steps. *cf accreting and amortising swaps*

Securitised asset swap

Another name for a *repackaged security*.

Special purpose vehicle

A one-off shell company, usually incorporated in a tax haven, set up to act as the issuer of a particular issue of repackaged securities. The SPV buys and holds the underlying assets and puts on a swap with the intermediary originating the repackaging, and then issues new securities which reflect the characteristics of the swapped asset. The proceeds of the new issue are used to fund the purchase of the assets being swapped and these are in turn used to collateralise the new issue. The SPV is legally separate from the intermediary originating the asset swap; the intermediary acts as the operating agent.

Spreadlock swap

An interest rate swap in which the swap spread is fixed immediately, but the benchmark yield can be fixed at the discretion of one of the counterparties at any time during an agreed period after the start of the swap. The end-user only has the right to choose *when* to fix the benchmark yield during the agreed period, not *if*: a spreadlock swap is therefore a 'time option'. Should the end-user fail to exercise its right to fix the benchmark yield by the end of the agreed period, it is fixed automatically.

Step-up/ step-down

Swaps with cash flows designed to match bonds — so-called *graduated* and *declining-coupon* bonds — which have coupons which increase or decrease in predetermined steps: in practice, there is usually just one step up or down.

Swaption

An option to enter into a forward swap in which the option-holder pays fixed interest. The term swaption is sometimes used for customer transactions and the term *callable swap* for interbank swaptions. A swaption tied to specific securities may be called a *contingent swap*.

Synthesis

The process in financial engineering in which the *unbundled* elements of a standard financial transaction are recombined into new permutations as new types of transaction. The process is also known as *repackaging*. The results are often labelled as *synthetic* or *hybrid* instruments.

Synthetic securities

In order to overcome the problems posed by *investor asset swaps*, intermediaries usually undertake the organisation of asset swaps on behalf of investors and take their place at the centre of the transactions. The asset being swapped is held by the intermediary for safe-keeping on behalf of the investor and the coupons are legally assigned to the intermediary in order to ensure it of the cash flows for the swap. As the investor only sees the swapped cash flow (not the actual flow from the underlying asset), as far as it is concerned, the asset which it has purchased is producing that cash flow directly. Because this is achieved by the intermediary combining the asset and swap, this structure is also known as a *packaged asset swap*. The advantages of this structure are:

■ the investor sees and is involved in the **administration** of only one cash flow;

■ the **credit risk** to which the investor is exposed is limited to that on the intermediary;

■ the **accounting** should be simplified, with the investor able to report the transaction as a single asset;

■ the intermediary can offer **liquidity** to the investor and there should only be a single transactions cost.

Terminable swap   Another name for a *putable swap*.

Unbundling   The financial engineering process of decomposing a standard financial transaction into its elements or *building blocks*, which can be:

■   forward contracts

■   option contracts

■   combinations of the two.

Zero-coupon swaps   An interest rate or currency swap in which all fixed interest payments (coupons) are deferred until maturity, while floating interest payments are made normally. An extreme form of *deferred-coupon swap*.

How to mark the self-study questions

Each of the questions has been awarded between 1 and 11 marks. The marks are set out in the table. Where questions have more than one part, fractions can be awarded. When all the marks have been added up, the results should be asessed against the distribution curve below.

Question	Part two	Part three
1	2	7
2	9	2
3	9	11
4	2	6
5	6	2
6	2	9
7	2	9
8	3	4
9	2	6
10	3	4
Total	**40**	**60**

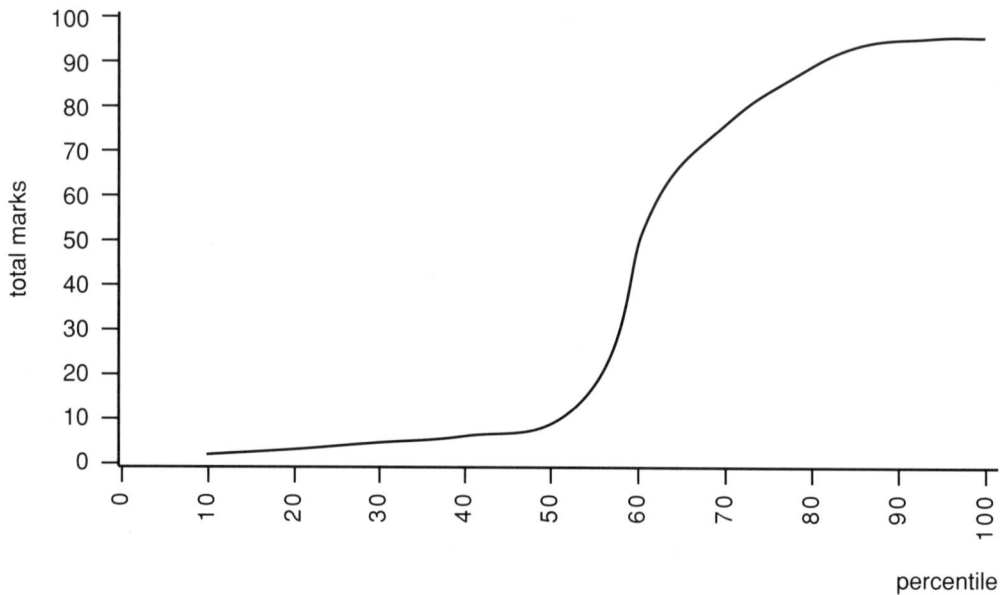

Percentile	Assessment
0—50%	You should start the Workbook again. Check that you work through it more methodically than before and in an environment conducive to study.
50—60%	You should think about re-reading the Workbook to reinforce your understanding of swaps. If you have lost marks in just one or two chapters, there is probably no need to re-read the whole Workbook, but you should go through the worked answers with care.
60—80%	A good result. You should think about skimming through the Workbook again to consolidate your knowledge.
80—100%	An excellent result. You should be able to progress quite easily to more specialised texts on swaps.

Coopers & Lybrand offices

Australia
D Prothero
Coopers & Lybrand Tower
580 George Street Sydney
New South Wales 2000
Tel: (03) 606 4500

Austria
H Wirth
Postfach 161
A 1092
Vienna
Tel: (1) 31377 0

Bahamas
C Johnson
PO Box N 596
Nassau NP
Tel: (809) 322 1061

Bahrain
F Ruttonsha
PO Box 787
Manama
Tel: (0973) 53007

Belgium
R Eeckhout
Marcel Thirty Court
Avenue Marcel Thirty 216
B-1200 Brussels
Tel: (02) 774 42 11

Bermuda
G Holmes
PO Box HM1171
Hamilton
Bermuda HMEX
Tel: (809) 295 2000

Brazil
P Baraldi
Caixa Postal 3168
CEP 01060
Sao Paulo
SP Brazil
Tel: (11) 530 0200

Canada
David Atkins
Aetna Canada Centre
145 King Street West
Toronto
Ontario
M5H 1V8
Tel: (416) 869 1130

Channel Islands
J Horrell
La Motte Chambers
St Helier
Jersey
Tel: (0534) 602000

Cyprus
D Papadopoulos
PO Box 1612
Nicosia
Tel: (02) 453053

Denmark
K Villadsen
PO Box 1443
DK 7500
Holstebro
Tel: (97-42) 19 88

Finland
M Tervo
PL 1015
00101
Helsinki
Tel: (0) 658 044

France
K Pilgrem
BP 451-08
75366 Paris
Cedex 08
Tel: (1) 44 20 80 00

Germany
H Wagener
Treuarbeit AG
Postfach 120
D-W 1000
Berlin 15
Tel: (030) 884 2020

Germany
K Lührig
Truehand-Vereiningung AG
Postfach 170 552
D-W 6000
Frankfurt am Main 1
Tel: (069) 71100

Hong Kong
R Chalmers
Sunning Plaza
10 Hysan Avenue
Hong Kong
Tel: 839 4321

Hungary
A Romer-Lee
PO Box 694
1539 Budapest
Tel: (1) 135 0140

Isle of Man
C Talavera
12 Finch Road
Douglas
Tel: (0624) 626711

Italy
P Barone
Via del Quirinale
00187 Rome
Tel: (0) 6 4744896

Japan
N Yamakoshi
Shin-Aoyama Bldg
Twin West 20F
1-1 Minami Aoyama 1-Chome
Minato-Ku
Tokyo 107
Tel: (3) 3475 1722

Leichtenstein
R Silvani
PO Box 1113
9490 Vaduz
Tel: 2 90 80

Luxembourg
M Chèvremont
BP 1446
L-1014
Luxembourg
Tel: 49749 1

Malaysia
M Abdullah
PO Box 10184
50706
Kuala Lumpur
Tel: (3) 441 1188

Malta
J Bonello
PO Box 61
Valleta Malta
Tel: 233648

Mexico
H Lara Silva
Apartado Postal 24-348
Col Roma
06700 Mexico
DF
Tel: (5) 208 1277

Netherlands
H Schaper
PO Bix 4200
1009 AE
Amsterdam
Tel: (20) 568 6666

New Zealand
R Hill
GPO Box 243
Wellington 6000
Tel: (4) 499 9898

Norway
E Westerby
Havnelageret
0150 Oslo 1
Tel: 02 40 00 00

Poland
D Thomas
Iwonicka 19
09-924 Warsaw
Tel: (22) 42 87 66

Portugal
C Bernardes
PO Box 1910
1004 Lisbon Codex
Tel: 793 0023

Rep of Ireland
B Cunningham
PO Box 1283
Dublin 2
Tel: (01) 610333

Rep of South Africa
R Barrow
PO Box 2536
Johannesburg 2000
Tel: (011) 498 4000

Russia
S Root
Ulinska Schchepkina 6
Moscow 129090
Tel: (095) 281 9466

Saudi Arabia
G Karaman
PO Box 2762
Riyad 11461
Tel: (01) 477 9504

Singapore
D Compton
Orchard PO Box 285
Singapore 9123
Tel: 336 2344

Spain
JJ Hierro
Apartado de Correos
36-191
28080 Madrid
Tel: (1) 572 0233

Sultanate of Oman
N Ferrand
PO Box 6075
Ruwi
Tel: 5637 17

Sweden
Johan Hafstrom
PO Box 27318
S-102 54 Stockholm
Tel: (8) 666 8000

Switzerland
R. Tschudi
Postfach 4152
CH 4002
Basel
(060) 277 5500

Thailand
N Charoentaveesub
GPO Box 788
Bangkok 10501
Tel: (2) 236 5227 9

Turkey
M Clarke
Buyukdere cad No 111
Kat; 2-3
Istanbul
Tel: (1) 175 2840

United Arab Emirates
H Nehme
PO Box 990
Abu Dhabi
Gayrettepe 80300
Tel: (02) 21123

United Kingdom
P. Reyniers
P.Rivett
London EC4A 4HT
Tel: (071) 583 5000

United States of America
C Jenkins
One Post Office Square
Boston
Massachusetts 02109
Tel: (617) 7574 5000

United States of America
W Van Rijn
1301 Avenue of the Americas
New York
NY 10019-6013
Tel: 259 7000